Foodie
BREAKS

> *ENGLAND, SCOTLAND, NORTHERN IRELAND, and WALES*

Foodie
BREAKS
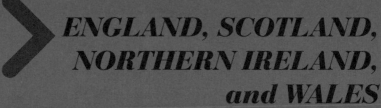
ENGLAND, SCOTLAND,
NORTHERN IRELAND,
and WALES

25 PLACES, 250 ESSENTIAL EATING EXPERIENCES

RICHARD MELLOR

DOG 'n' BONE

About the author

A self-described "gun for hire," Richard Mellor is a freelance travel and food journalist who writes regularly for *Metro, The Times, The Guardian, Telegraph Online,* the *Evening Standard,* and *Broadly.* This is the follow-up to Richard's first book, *Foodie City Breaks: Europe.* He is based in London, UK.

Published in 2020 by Dog 'n' Bone Books
An imprint of Ryland Peters & Small Ltd
20–21 Jockey's Fields   341 E 116th St
London WC1R 4BW   New York, NY 10029

www.rylandpeters.com

10 9 8 7 6 5 4 3 2 1

A CIP catalog record for this book is available from the Library of Congress and the British Library.

ISBN: 978 1 912983 00 1

Printed in China

Designer: Jerry Goldie

Commissioning editor: Kate Burkett
Art director: Sally Powell
Production controller: David Hearn
Publishing manager: Penny Craig
Publisher: Cindy Richards

Contents

Introduction

These past two decades have seen a new word flood the British travel sphere. Cape Town or the Caribbean be damned; suddenly domestic "staycations" are just as desirable, and far, far trendier. Nor is this staycation train showing any sign of slowing down: a recent trend report from travel association ABTA revealed that 56 percent of Brits are now planning a holiday in the UK.

Such a swelling in popularity for British breaks has been much encouraged by various factors, including a fondness for all things retro, a desire to fly less in the name of eco-friendliness, and, yes, pre-Brexit financial gloom. The latter has also caused the sterling to depreciate against many foreign currencies, including the euro and the US dollar, and thus encouraged floods of canny, bargain-seeking tourists to UK shores.

And, helping everything along has been the quiet resurgence of British food. The land of Lancashire hotpots and beans on toast is now a culinary heavyweight, with grub one of the main reasons to visit—or to staycation—in itself.

Leading the way, naturally, is London: the capital's long-standing legendary restaurants have recently earned rivals in further northern, southern, western, and eastern reaches, from Canonbury car garages and Cointreau yogurt in Walthamstow to Crystal Palace's coffee gem and cheap Crofton Park pizzerias, and this guide devotes a section to each area accordingly.

Other cities are fast catching up. Birmingham's best restaurants deliver haddock and eggs with cornflakes and curry oil or delicate quail samosas. In Manchester an understated Japanese gem plays bebop, while Edinburgh is home to the most tolerant Indian diner around. Delve deep into Liverpool and you'll find Britain's best breakfast whereas Belfast boasts buoyant coffee and cocktail scenes.

Classic holiday regions such as the Lake District, the New Forest, Bath, and the Norfolk coast have also upped their gastro game, and so, too, has Brighton, which stands on the cusp of southern England's sparkling wine revolution, and cool towns Margate and Deal along the Kent coast.

Then there are the secret places, bubbling deliciously under the radar. You've possibly not

even heard of Malton or Castle Douglas, while the public's awareness of County Down and Aberdeenshire tends to be low. All four—and their acclaimed macaroons, craft-beer crawls, and champion cheeses—feature here, however.

I hope that this book will prove useful. Places will close and chefs will change but, by and large, the suggestions here ought to be timeless and trustworthy. Wherever you go, raise a toast to Britain and its newfound epicurean prowess.

Richard Mellor

The Places

Cromer

and surrounding areas

ENGLAND

> With due respect to the rest of Norfolk—and the particularly likeable city Norwich, which has some great places to feed—a bevy of fine food clusters in the county's north. From Waxham to The Wash, in between epic sandy beaches and uber-chichi market towns, await vanilla veloutés, soft curd cheeses, and purveyors of the famous Cromer Crab, both along the coast and inland.

ON A BUDGET?

As well as making TV appearances and cooking at the Michelin-starred Morston Hall restaurant, Galton Blackiston oversees seaside *No1 Cromer* in the gentrified Victorian clifftop resort town. And while Upstairs at No1 is a posh chippie and Downstairs is mid-range in price, the takeaway option hawks cod and chips combos for a bargain £7.50. Just along the coast in Sheringham, which retains a more traditional feel, the simple-looking *Roy Boys* serves high-quality café fare: bacon baguettes here come with stilton, and salads include a zesty crab option. Gluten- and dairy-free options are available and warm service is guaranteed.

New Street (+44 1263 515983, www.no1cromer.com); 37 Station Road (+44 1263 822960)

SPLASH OUT

In Stanhoe near Burnham Market *The Duck Inn* looks like a house, sounds like a pub, and, with most mains the wrong side of £20, levies like a ritzy restaurant. Such prices seem far fairer once Ben Handley's awards and well-sourced seasonal fare are considered however, and especially after you cut into treacle-cured beef fillets alongside mustard cream cheese or devour cod cheeks supported by chorizo, cockles, and vanilla velouté. Costlier still is **The Neptune Inn**, an unfussy Michelin-starred haunt in coastal Old Hunstanton known for such holy combos as suckling pig, pak choi, sweet potato, and red pepper purée.

Burnham Road (+44 1485 518330, www.duckinn.co.uk); 85 Old Hunstanton Road (+44 1485 532122, www.theneptune.co.uk)

PUB PERFECTION

The Wiveton Bell is only a few miles inland from Blakeney Point National Nature Reserve and its gray seal colony—who breed impossibly cute white pups here in winter. Pints of Yetman's and Woodforde's Wherry can be supped inside a beamed but rather formal interior, or out in the garden. Not far west sprawls Norfolk's best beach, Holkham Bay, an expanse of sand, space, waves, and pine-wooded dunes. The best blustery strolls here conclude in the same estate's ivy-covered **Victoria Inn**, crammed with Indian antiques. As well as nice bedrooms and fine food, its restful bar stocks handpicked wines and beers.

Blakeney Road (+44 1263 740101, www.wivetonbell.co.uk); Park Road (+44 1328 711008, www.holkham.co.uk/stay-eat/the-victoria-inn)

REGIONAL FAVES

There's no doubting Norfolk's most famous delicacy. Cromer crabs are no different in biology to the rest of Britain's brown crabs, but their shallow chalk-reef home causes a flavor so sweet and succulent that it's protected by law. April through October is the main season and **The Old Rock Shop Bistro** is the best place to taste. Another decorated seaside bounty in these parts are Brancaster mussels: especially juicy, big, and tender mollusc harvested off Brancaster Beach. **The White Horse Inn**, along the coast at Brancaster Straithe, cooks them five different ways during all-day Mussel Mondays.

10 Hamilton Road (+44 1263 511926, www.theoldrockshopbistro.co.uk); Main Road (+44 1485 210262, www.whitehorsebrancaster.co.uk)

▼ The chalk shelf and nutrient-rich waters in north Norfolk make for a particularly flavorsome, tender, and fragrant crab.

BEST FEST

At the heart of the Holkham Estate stands Holkham Hall, an eighteenth-century beauty built in picturesque Palladian style. Just as attractive is its high-walled garden, which hosts the annual *North Norfolk Food & Drink Festival*—usually across the first weekend in September. Against a backdrop of red bricks, local producers will sell their best beers, breads, pies, and pralines alongside children's face-painting stalls and a hexagonal cookery theater tent used for demos. A fall alternative is provided by the *Aylsham Food Festival*, held in October amid the more-southerly River Bure town and involving cheese tastings and a Sunday brunch for 100 people.

www.northnorfolkfoodfestival.co.uk; www.slowfoodaylsham.org.uk

SUITCASE SWAG

Burnham Market's nickname of "Chelsea-on-Sea" says it all about this picture-postcard, *Conde Nast Traveller*-reading town, one whose Georgian green is flanked by beckoning food shops. Just as handsome though, but in a seaside, flint-and-brick way, is Cley. Here, along with an emblematic windmill-turned-B&B, you'll find the family-run *Cley Smokehouse*, its oak-scented shop full of superlative kippers, shrimp, and crab pâtés to buy. A few doors down, the *Picnic Fayre* delicatessen majors in charcuterie and also cheeses by prize-hoovering local legend

Catherine (AKA Mrs) Temple. Her Wensleydale-like Walsingham and Wighton soft curd both make for excellent purchases.

High Street (+44 1263 740282, www.cleysmokehouse.com); High Street (+44 1263 740587, www.picnic-fayre.co.uk)

BEER OH BEER

Question: which UK county has the most microbreweries? The answer, as you probably guessed, is Norfolk, with its warm climate and salty sea air forging a moreish malting barley. Two of the best brewers are based in the high fields north of Norwich. Utilizing a new borehole for ultra-fresh water, Buxton's *Wildcraft Brewery* makes five regular beers, plus seasonal, hedgerow-foraged specials. Tasting tours run on selected Saturdays. Over at Reepham, *Panther Brewery*—its name inspired by alleged local sightings of the feline—sells its award-winning stout and hoppy red, golden, and pale ales from an onsite shop.

Foragers' Rest, Coltishall Road (+44 1603 278054, www.wildcraftbrewery.co.uk); Unit 1, Collers Way (+44 7766 558215, www.pantherbrewery.co.uk)

▲ The Cley Smokehouse is famous for its kippers, which are slowly cold-smoked over oak in a traditional brick kiln oven.

☕ CAFFEINE KICKS

In 2012, inspired by coffee culture's growth around the globe, *Grey Seal*— named after those blubbery mammals at nearby Blakeney—decided to bring specialty roasting to Glandford, a small village on the North Norfolk coast. How, they wondered, would the local terroir influence beans from Thailand to Costa Rica? Delectably, as it turns out. Awards and acclaim have flooded in and there are now Grey Seal coffee shops in Wells-next-the-Sea, Blakeney itself, Sheringham, and Cromer. Only at the original roastery however, will you also find a vegan café and two bakeries in former shipping containers.

Manor Farm Barns (+44 1263 740249, www.greysealcoffee. co.uk)

🍴 BRILL FOR BRUNCH

Another of northern Norfolk's poster boys, Holt is an effortlessly pretty Georgian town replete with rummageable boutiques and well-trimmed hedges. It's a lovely place to linger and nowhere suits mid-morning lingers better than *Byfords*, a guesthouse, store, and farmhouse-style café in one. Offered until 11.30am from Monday through Saturday and until 3pm on Sundays, the

▲ Occupying what is believed to be the Georgian town of Holt's oldest building, Byford's offers generous brunch portions for both locals and guests of this self-proclaimed "posh B&B."

latter's breakfast menu spans smoothies, scrambled egg, and smoked salmon-stuffed croissants, kippers, kedgeree, smashed avocado on muffins, homemade cinnamon rolls, and even a breakfast pizza topped with beans, sausage, bacon, black pudding, egg, mushroom, and—this being pizza— mozzarella. Phew.

1–3 Shirehall Plain (+44 1263 711400, www.byfords.org.uk)

🥂 DATE FOR TWO

"Anything for love." So, encouragingly, reads original neon lettering by none other than Tracey Emin at the *Gunton Arms*. A hunting lodge turned country pub with rooms south of Cromer, the Gunton's a rare beast indeed, lining informal, crackling-fire lounges with high-value modern art. Also present are Damien Hirst butterflies, Gilbert & George prints, and, to really set the mood, erotic shots by Japanese photographer Nobuyoshi. It all makes for a memorable date, as does artisanal tuck—be it Cromer crabs or venison from the surrounding deer park— cooked earthily by Stuart Tattersall, previously a head chef under Mark Hix.

Cromer Road (+44 1263 832010, theguntonarms.co.uk)

Southwold, Aldeburgh,

and surrounding areas

ENGLAND

> One glimpse at East Suffolk's sprawl of oh-so-arable, farm-studded fields and you immediately understand why the nosh is so good here. Then there's the fast-eroding coastline, which throws in fresh fish and delectable oysters. It all makes for a fantastic short break when combined with the area's Norman castles, beaches, gone-posh towns like Southwold, and thriving arts scene.

💰 ON A BUDGET?

The world's best chippy is how some describe *Aldeburgh Fish & Chips*, which has been run by the same family since they bought it from a Mr Cooper—no first name, apparently—in 1967. It's no wonder that today's queues routinely stretch around the corner with sensational, fresh-off-the-line seafood and proper potato fries. Ditto the prices: even if you order the biggest haddock and largest portion of chips, you still won't spend a tenner. Most eat their meal from the bag on Aldeburgh's classic shingle waterfront as rollers come in, the backdrop formed by elegant buildings in vibrant pastel shades.

226 High Street (+44 1728 452250, www. aldeburghfishandchips.co.uk)

🔔 SPLASH OUT

Follow the River Alde south and you come to an even prettier village, Orford, home to a lonely twelfth-century polygonal castle. Close by the English Channel, from whose beds Pinney's plucks oh-so-juicy oysters for its shop, is nearby *Butley Orford Oysterage* restaurant. Scoff homemade strawberry meringue afterward. More dining options await at *The Swan* in Southwold, another coastal town to the north.

◀ Aldeburgh Fish & Chips has earned the accolade of "best fish and chips in England" from singer Ed Sheeran.

▲ More than just a hotel, The Swan is a place where you can enjoy a quick coffee, tasty meal, or a relaxing week away.

At the front of its gone-boutique Georgian coach-house, The Still Room serves such locally inspired fare as dry-aged venison loin with five-day fermented barley, Adnams rye-malt whiskey, and chocolate, all as demijohn wall-lights lend a coppery glow.

Market Hill (+44 1394 450277, www.pinneysoforford.co.uk/ restaurant); Market Place (+44 1502 722186, www.theswansouthwold.co.uk)

PUB PERFECTION

You might need a pint after visiting Sutton Hoo, where a new full-size replica sculpture of the 27-meter, treasure-stuffed Anglo-Saxon ship burial discovered here in 1939 has been installed. One mile across less disturbed fields, in Bromeswell, is *The Unruly Pig*, a beamed beauty that recently earned *Good Pub Guide* plaudits for both its food and wine. Lunch menus include sardines on toast and warm duck Caesar salads. Waveney Valley walkers, meanwhile, should direct their muddy boots to Bramfield and *The Queen's Head*, a refurbished sixteenth-century watering hole, which does a good line in sandwiches, sharing boards, and burgers.

▼ The Unruly Pig prides itself on local, and seasonal British food with an Italian twist.

Orford Road (+44 1394 460310, www.theunrulypig.co.uk); The Street (+44 1986 784214, www. queensheadbramfield.co.uk)

REGIONAL FAVES

Suffolk is famed for its delectable strawberries and raspberries, which brighten up British summers and supermarkets. Happily, there are still pick-your-own (PYO) farms to peruse. One of the best is *Friday Street Farm*, south of Saxmundham, where orchards are accompanied by a café where those same fruits inform raspberry roulades and Victoria sponges. Further east, in a village of the same name, Aspall's makes its acclaimed cyder—the "y" indicating that it has been fermented twice for a stronger taste. Visitors aren't allowed, so get a pint in nearby village Debenham's excellent, tomato-colored *Woolpack* pub instead.

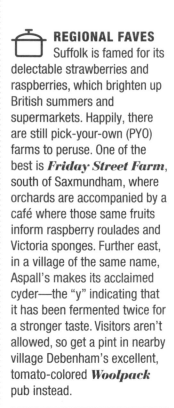

Friday Street, just off A1094 (+44 1728 602783, www.fridaystfarm. co.uk); 49 High Street (+44 1728 860516, www.sites.google.com/ site/thedebenhamwoolpack)

BRILL FOR BRUNCH

A bumper three options are on offer here as Suffolk excels at brunch. Back amid Orford's flint cottages, the *Pump Street*

Bakery's small caff majors in magnificent sourdough bread and smoky-bacon brioche buns. There's Monmouth coffee, too, from a machine called Percy. Inland at Framlingham, handsomely facing its church, *The Lemon Tree* does all the classics plus veggie croquettes, determinedly using Suffolk fare. And up in Weston, near Beccles and its heated riverside lido, *The Café at Urban Jungle* is a tropical, palm-swathed, plant-nursery den doing everything from shakshuka to vegan quiche—and doing it very well.

1 Pump Street (+44 1394 459829, www.pumpstreetchocolate.com); 3 Church Street (+44 1728 621232, www.facebook.com/ lemontreefram); London Road (+44 1502 559103, www.urbanjungle.co.uk/cafes/ suffolk-cafe/)

▲ Built by local craftsmen in 1728, The Cyder House in the village of Aspall still houses Clement Chevallier's original mill and press.

◄ Be sure to make a pit stop at this family-owned bakery and café to sample their outstanding bread and handmade pastries.

🍺 BEER OH BEER

Though ciders, wines, spirits, and even kitchenware are produced at *Adnams'* brewery and distillery in seaside Southwold, beers have been the focus ever since it opened in 1872. Cucumelon Sour is currently the oddball offering, while citrus ale Ghost Ship boasts most fame. Ninety-minute brewery tours run each afternoon for £20, concluding with tastings and a free drink. Elsewhere, the ferry port of Lowestoft boasts Britain's most easterly brewery, Green Jack, with an onsite tavern serving its real ales, while Ipswich's best beer pub is the *Fat Cat* free house, thanks to its 20+ cask ales.

Market Place (+44 1502 727200, www.adnams.co.uk); 288 Spring Road (+44 1473 726524, www.fatcatipswich.co.uk)

▲ An award-winning UK brewer, Adnams brewery produces everything from cask ales, wines, and spirits to kitchenware.

☕ CAFFEINE KICKS

Another Ipswich place worth investigating is *Applaud Coffee*, run by sisters Beth and Hannah. Freshly baked scones and breakfasts are also served, perhaps in the courtyard garden, but the relevant product for this section is home produced and single origin guest espresso blends, all manipulated excellently in the Saints-quarter shop. Equally adept are the baristas of *Honey* + *Harvey* in Woodbridge, who use beans from Bury St Edmunds roaster Butterworth & Son plus La Marzocco, FB80, and Mythos One kit. The food offering runs to crispy chicken wings with blue cheese sauce and house-smoked BBQ pork ribs with pickled red slaw.

19 St Peter's Street (+44 1473 808142, www.applaud-coffee.co.uk); 56 Thoroughfare (+44 1394 547216, www.honeyandharvey.co.uk/woodbridge)

◀ Choose to have smoked kippers transformed into a delicious dish by the kitchen at The Farm Café & Shop or buy them from the shop next door.

SUITCASE SWAG

Not only does the *Farm Café + Shop* in Marlesford, north of Woodbridge, serve smoked Pinney's kippers and vegan cooked breakfasts, but its store is heaven for hamper-fillers. Among the local fare on sale are chutneys and cheeses. If you're a firm adherent to the "bigger is better" philosophy however, head to Wherstead just south of Ipswich, and the 8,000-square-foot *Suffolk Food Hall*—a converted cattle barn where butchers, bakers, chocolatiers, and gin distillers hawk their stuff. It's basically a glorified farmers' market. The onsite Cookhouse restaurant, looking onto the River Orwell, is good for lunch.

Main Road (A12) (+44 1728 747717, www.farmcafe.co.uk/shop); Wherstead, off B1456 (+44 1473 786610, www.suffolkfoodhall.co.uk)

TEA TIME

Here are your instructions for the *Southwold Boating Lake Tearoom* just inland from the sea. Don't sit down in its tiny, forties-style waterside caff nor in the Lloyd Loom chairs on a waterside veranda. Instead, ask to have your sweet or savory cream tea on one of the islands, amid birds and boaters. Hot scones and buttery toasted teacakes are the norm. Just as

quirky is the alfresco *Blue Rabbit Cafe*, part of a smallholding in Shottisham. All the organic fruit cakes, cookies, oat bars, and brownies are made by owner Claire, whose alpacas you might also meet.

North Parade (+44 7771 781739, www.southwoldboating lakeandtearoom.co.uk); Shottisham Campsite (+44 7867 488955, www.bluerabbitcafe.com)

BEST FEST

The *Aldeburgh Food & Drink Festival* starts over a late-September weekend with demos, talks, and tastings before rippling out over a series of fringe events across the following fortnight. In 2019, luminaries attending the main bash—held at the

▲ A celebration of Suffolk's thriving food and drink scene, Aldeburgh Food & Drink Festival sees over 100 local producers take part.

music and arts campus Snape Maltings, which also hosts a monthly farmers' market—included Christmas Bake-Off winner and YouTube star, Chetna Makan, and food writer, Thomasina Miers, while subsequent offerings spanned macaron masterclasses and the annual Great Framlingham Sausage Festival, in which attendees vote a winning banger as bands play.

www.aldeburghfoodanddrink.co.uk

North London

ENGLAND

> Rather like its southern counterpart, North London has a slightly low brow rep. But that only makes it sweeter when one finds the Chinese gem in Drayton Park, the French toast with Cointreau yogurt in Walthamstow, the romantic bistro in West Hampstead, and the Italian-inspired tapas served in a former Canonbury car garage.

💲 ON A BUDGET?

While most footie fans attending Arsenal games at the Emirates Stadium opt for pies, burgers, or a sausage roll, the savviest head to three quality haunts around Drayton Park. And while *Wolkite's* *kitfo* beef and pulse stews from Ethiopia, and the Ghanaian joint *Sweet Handz'* fried plantains, jollof rice, and fatty turkey tail are reasonably priced, *Xian Impression's* dishes from China's northerly Shaanxi province are a *total* steal. Look for its chunky, hand-pulled *biang biang* noodles, lashed with Sichuan peppercorns, and *rou jia mo*: flatbread stuffed with pork or beef.

82 Hornsey Road (+44 20 7700 3055, www.wolkiterestaurant. com); 217 Holloway Road (+44 20 7700 6427, www.sweethandz.co. uk); 117 Benwell Road (+44 20 3441 0191, www.xianimpression. co.uk)

🔔 SPLASH OUT

One of Britain's most exciting chefs is now on Upper Street, Islington's rangy, restaurant-obsessed main street. *Great British Menu's* champion of champions, James Cochran uses his unusual heritage—Caribbean and Scottish ancestry, and a childhood in Whitstable—at *12:51*, explaining such exotic concoctions as oysters with eucalyptus or braised goat shoulder enlivened by pumpkin, cumin, and coconut. Much more old-school are the legendary restaurateurs Corbin & King and their latest venture is in well-to-do St John's Wood, beside Regent's Park. *Soutine* is a stately, Parisian-style brasserie delivering comfort food such as coq au Riesling or steak tartare under a quail's egg.

107 Upper St (+44 7934 202269, www.1251.co.uk); 60 St John's Wood High Street (+44 20 3926 8448, www.soutine.co.uk)

▲▶ Inspired by the cafés of Paris, Soutine is a beautiful brasserie that is open throughout the day for breakfast, brunch, lunch, and dinner. Dishes include eggs benedict, croque madame, and confit de canard.

KILLER COCKTAILS

Just off Upper Street, **The Four Sisters** is a laid-back, cozy alternative to pricier Islington cocktail bars like 69 Colebrooke Row. It's also, arguably, better: here you'll find lavender and passion fruit syrups made in house, more specially infused tinctures than a typical chemist, and hundreds of spirits. You can order classics—including six-week, barrel aged negronis and elderflower juleps—or tell the bartenders your

▲ The all-vegetarian Buhler & Co offers a diverse range of dishes, from quinoa cakes to pad Thai tofu, all of which are super-healthy.

preferences and let them tailor something. Go on a school night if possible; this dark, Dickensian den can get a bit too busy and rowdy on weekends. A sibling has opened in the City, but it doesn't compare.

25 Canonbury Lane (+44 20 7226 0955, www.foursistersbars.com)

BRILL FOR BRUNCH

Headed to Walthamstow? Reasons to ride the Victoria Line to its northeastern most stop include a museum devoted to all-round creative William Morris, Europe's longest street market, and **Buhler & Co**, who prove once more that Antipodeans really do do brunch best. The all-vegetarian

8 Chingford Road (+44 20 8527 3652, www.buhlerandco.com); 5 Stable Street (+44 20 7420 9321, www.dishoom.com/kings-cross)

💬 LOCAL SECRET

Part of *Primeur's* charm comes from its unlikely location in a former car garage deep in residential, leafy Canonbury, surrounded by flat shares and dog walkers. Then there's the food. Now boasting two siblings—the seafood sequel Westerns Laundry, located in an ex-Lower Holloway laundrette, and all-day bakery restaurant Jolene on nearby Newington Green—it serves Italian-inspired tapas and many natural wines. The vibe is easy-going, and the nosh superb. So too are the unique treats—quince and custard Danish pastries and maple

options mean everything is healthy; it's just that some things (roast baby potatoes, pad Thai tofu, and mange tout) are healthier than others (chocolate French toast, roast plum, and Cointreau yogurt). Down in Kings Cross' rebooted Granary Square area, revered Bombay-style café chain **Dishoom** uses a typically big, typically beautiful, typically charismatic space for its sausage naans and spicy, fragrant sweet chais.

▲ Pophams strives to create new and exciting flavor combinations with its pastries.

bacon swirls—and gourmet hot chocs of *Pophams*, an Islington bakery–café also found at Centre Point's new food court (see *West London*, pages 26–31).

116 Petherton Road (+44 20 7226 5271, www.primeurn5.co.uk); 19 Prebend Street (www.pophamsbakery.com)

🍷 PERPETUAL WINE

Open since 1971, *Cork & Bottle* is undoubtedly a terrific old school wine bar, but Leicester Square still seems a strange location. A bit mainstream, no? In 2017 a new sister venue in Paddington puzzled further. A bit gritty, no? One year later sense prevailed, and a third outpost has arrived in the altogether more suitable surrounds of Hampstead. Amid its leafy streets and handsome heath is the former White Horse pub, now rebooted into a 300-bottle wine extravaganza stocking some of the world's most treasured plonk. Along with the wine, there are garlic-stuffed snails, steaks, and signature ham and cheese pies to wolf down.

154–156 Fleet Street (+44 20 7267 6484, www.thecorkandbottle.co.uk/hampstead)

PUB PERFECTION

Islington's Georgian backstreets hide brilliant pubs: The Albion and its huge garden, George Orwell's fave, The Compton Arms, and its burger pop-up, the canal side Narrowboat and, close to City Road, the tropical *Island Queen*. An old gin palace with dark woods and palm trees around an island bar, this den does unusual cocktails and buttermilk chicken burgers with easy, unpretentious flair. The only people unimpressed may be the craft beer fanatics, who are instead directed to *The Southampton Arms* for 20+ draught options from UK microbreweries. Between sips, why not ponder the pub's curious location: it's not quite in Gospel Oak, Tufnell Park, or Kentish Town.

87 Noel Road (+44 20 7354 8741, www.theislandqueenislington. co.uk); 139 Highgate Road (www. thesouthamptonarms.co.uk)

CAFFEINE KICKS

Even as little as ten years ago, North Londoners had to head south in order to find artisan coffee. Now, however, there are good places everywhere from Archway to Finchley Road. Representing the former is *Bread and Bean*, where Union Coffee beans are expertly put through a La Marzocco machine as freelancers work on brown leather banquettes next to colorful geometric wallpaper. As for Finchley Road, close to the tube station about halfway up you'll find the diminutive,

South Korean-run *Loft Coffee Company*, which serves brunch plates alongside carefully sourced Square Mile and Crankhouse blends.

37 Junction Road (+44 20 7263 0667, www.facebook.com/ breadandbean); 4 Canfield Gardens (+44 20 7372 2008, www. facebook.com/loftcoffeecompany)

DATE FOR TWO

Posh boutiques and an affluent feel render West Hampstead nice for a date— and *Hãm* helps further. Meaning "home" in Old English, the name is apt given this bistro's exposed red brick and low lights. The imaginative, daily changing menus—modern British fare using produce carefully sourced from across

▲ Selling products from small independent UK breweries, The Southampton Arms has 18 taps full of lovely ale and cider.

▶ Loft Coffee Company uses great beans perfectly brewed, which has caffeine fans flocking.

the land—from ex-Ledbury chef Matt Osborne also seduces. In *Hicce*, a restaurant atop Wolf & Badger in King's Cross' redeveloped Coal Drops Yard warehouse, pot plants and Shaker-style chairs accompany shareable comfort food with a Japanese touch from another "Great British Menu" star, Pip Lacey.

238 West End Lane (+44 20 7813 0168, www.hamwesthampstead. com); 102 Stable Street (+44 20 3869 8200, www.hicce.co.uk)

MARKET RESEARCH

At the top of Clerkenwell—and therefore just about eligible for this category if we bend the geographical rules— pedestrianized *Exmouth Market* has gentrified fast in recent years, with acclaimed epicurean names such as Caravan, Mother Clucker, and Pizza Pilgrims opening outlets. Then there's ever busy gastropub The Eagle and coffee purveyors Grind. Weekdays see the happy addition of stalls selling street food in the middle, from Travestere's tomatoey beef stews to burritos with ancho peppers and refried beans at Freebird. Look out, too, for tiny Cafe Kick, London's premier foosball bar.

www.exmouth.london

▲▼ A neighborhood restaurant, Hām creates simple but imaginative modern British cuisine using quality ingredients.

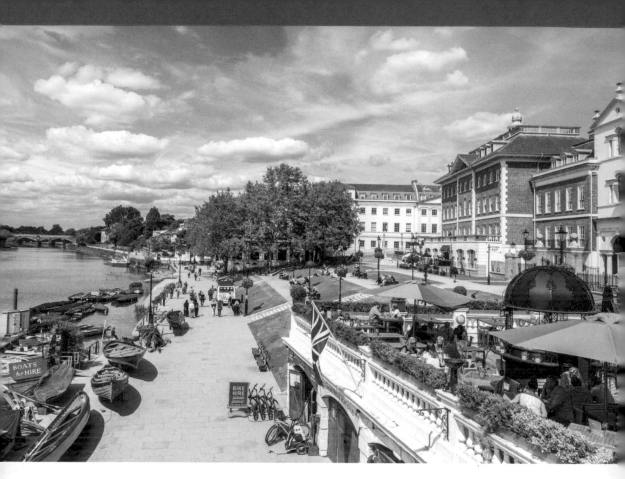

West London

ENGLAND

> When divvying up London, this book opted to (mostly) obey the capital's postcodes—forcing this section to cover everything between Richmond and the Royal Opera House. Within these pages, therefore, are Algerian sandwich stalls, Asian cocktail dens, TripAdvisor redemption stories, and corner pubs containing hidden worlds.

ON A BUDGET?

Amid the exotic mayhem of Shepherd's Bush Market, whose traders and fans recently resisted Boxpark's arrival, is *Sam Sandwiches*, a stall where Algerian alchemy is allowed free reign. Having chosen two freshly prepared fillings, such as merguez sausage or kofte lamb, customers see their light bread concoction first get fried with eggs and chips, and then expertly spiced up using tangy harissa and mayo. The results are life-changing. Over in Queensway, Malaysian café *Normah's* serves sea bass in tamarind juice or pandan leaf rice with peanut-flavored beef rendang for a song—spending a tenner is hard—and always with a big smile to boot.

9 Shepherd's Bush Market; 23–25 Queensway Market (+44 7340 294660, www.normahs.co.uk)

SPLASH OUT

Why should vegetarian restaurants be bargain priced? A lack of meat needn't mean a lack of quality: Notting Hill's plant based *Farmacy*, for instance, sources high-end produce from biodynamic, small batch farms for its artichoke pizzettas and Middle Eastern bowls and bills them accordingly. Ignore the snarky reviews from snarky critics: the clean eating wave was always going to earn some baseless bounce back. If carnivorousness is non-negotiable, however, head to the best of London's star chef hotel restaurants. At *Kerridge's Bar & Grill* inside Charing Cross' swanky Corinthia, Tom Kerridge twists chickens and beef in a central

▶ The team from the Hand & Flowers in Marlow have brought their passion and produce to this legendary venue in the form of Kerridge's Bar & Grill.

rotisserie, and serves them with lardo or garlic-charged hispi cabbage.

74 Westbourne Grove (+44 20 7221 0705, www.farmacylondon. com); 10 Northumberland Avenue (+44 20 7321 3244, www.kerridgesbarandgrill.co.uk)

MARKET RESEARCH

Despite being one of London's first skyscrapers, Oxford Street's famous Centre Point has endured long-term vacancy and demolition threats. Suddenly, though, it is home to the capital's hottest mini market hall of them all. Ground

floor *Arcade Food Theatre* collates cult providers: options include Tātā Eatery's katsu sandos and Yorkshire pudding and steak wraps from Flat Iron. A cheaper, more exotic, and more epicurean alternative to nearby Portobello, Notting Hill's frenzied *Golborne Road Market* stars Trinidadian roti wrap and Moroccan tagine stalls, with the surrounding shops headlined by Portuguese deli caff Lisboa and its patisserie opposite. Fridays and Saturdays are best.

103–105 New Oxford Street (+44 20 7519 1202, www. arcade-london.com); Golborne Road (www.rbkc.gov.uk)

PUB PERFECTION

Wandering deeper inside West Brompton corner pub *The Prince,* it's easy to think you've drunk too much and unwittingly entered some sort of street food Narnia. Uh-uh: this series of interconnected old townhouses, their chicken or taco vendors, and central, retractable roof garden are actually a semi-secret market type adaptation. Part of that takeover involved a makeover: the original Victorian boozer was given a brass and marble tart up. Elsewhere, those who'll travel anywhere for a good Sunday roast are directed to Fulham's riverside *The Crabtree*. The top-notch carcasses being cooked here include Gloucester Old Spot pork bellies, Suffolk barn-reared chickens, and 28-day aged Angus beef rumps.

14 Lillie Road (+44 7496 584766, www.theprincelondon.com); 4 Rainville Road (+44 20 7385 3929, www.thecrabtreew6.co.uk)

BRILL FOR BRUNCH

North of the Westway, Queen's Park is a low-profile residential area full of nice corners. One such, down a cobbled mews, is bright, white walled café and wine bar *Milk Beach*. Brunch here is great, whether it involves poke bowls, banana bread under espresso cream cheese, or smashed avocado and whipped goats' cheese on Little Bread Pedlar sourdough. Or indeed Neal's Yard organic yogurt plus homemade honey granola fruit, or coddled eggs in a jar with cream, sweet potato purée, and sourdough soldiers. One of the co-owners is a

former UK Roasting Champion, so you're guaranteed good coffee, too.

19 Lonsdale Road (+44 20 8144 8277, www.milkbeach.com)

BEER OH BEER

London's best bottle shop? A prime contender is Fulham's *DR.iNK*, a friendly boutique whose high wooden shelves and fridges are stocked to capacity with 600+ options—everything from Beavertown and Brick to By The Horns and BrewYork. You'll find special collaborative efforts as well, and rare quirks such as Cave Creek Chili Beer. On Saturday, visitors are invited to chow vegetarian samosas in store while supping brews on the front patio. If a pub vibe is preferable, wander into under the radar Pimlico and find *Cask Pub & Kitchen*. The original Craft Beer Co premises, it has 25 rotating poisons on tap.

349 Fulham Palace Road (+44 20 7610 6795, www.drinkoffulham. com); 6 Charlwood Street (+44 20 7630 7225, www. caskpubandkitchen.com)

◀ A café and wine bar, Milk Beach sources speciality coffees and organic and natural wines from around the world.

KILLER COCKTAILS

You'll need to don smarts and shiny shoes, but Mayfair's *Connaught Bar* is worth dressing up for. Within shimmering, black art deco surrounds, Agostino Perrone prepares triumphant Connaught Martinis using bespoke bitters from a trolley. From. A. Trolley. His eventual libation easily merits the faff, and considerable expense. Across

▲ As well as their killer cocktails, Wun's also offers an abundance of brunch, lunch, and dinner dishes.

Regent Street, Soho's ever-expanding clump of cocktail dens is led by *Wun's*, below a Chinese tearoom and mimicking mid-century Hong Kong speakeasies. Open on weekends until "very late," it proposes blends from sweet— bamboo fenjiu, tea liqueur, quince, and mango—to sour,

including plum-infused baiju, plum tea, liquorice, and five spice syrup.

Carlos Place (+44 20 7499 7070, www.the-connaught.co.uk); 23 Greek Street (+44 20 8017 9888, www.tearoom.bar)

TIME FOR TEA

There are two types of London tearoom. First comes the posh, tiered tray kind. Claridge's, Fortnum & Mason, and The Wolseley are all classic and worthy afternoon tea shouts but, for something more forward-thinking, try the **Berners Tavern** in Fitzrovia. Jason Atherton oversees things here, explaining constituents like mustard and cider cured ham croissants, caramel macaroons, and toasted crumpets with brown shrimp and caviar. The second type is a charming, dainty china kind.

▲ Enjoy afternoon tea, amongst other meals, in the stylish surrounds of Berners Tavern.

Leading the charge here is *Tea and Tattle* whose scones, sandwiches, lemon drizzle cake, and loose-leaf cha can be found in the Oriental-themed basement of an independent Bloomsbury bookshop opposite the British Museum.

10 Berners St (+44 20 7908 7979, www.bernerstavern.com); 41 Great Russell Street (+44 7722 192703, www.teaandtattle.com)

CAFFEINE KICKS

With respect to the considerable claims of Clerkenwell, Fitzrovia is also London's premier destination for coffee pilgrims. It boasts a surplus of the kind of semi ascetic places where ordering a cappuccino is roughly akin to insulting the owner's mother. Such pre-eminence was proven recently when two more cult java joints chose to open here, despite Kaffeine, Workshop, and co already being in situ.

First to arrive were Japanese legends Omotesando Koffee, a bespoke Assembly blend accompanying their stark pale wood decor and high-tech wizardry. Then followed a reprise—rare filters, quality snacks, bright surrounds—of Richmond's surprise smash *Kiss The Hippo*.

8 Newman Street (www.ooo-koffee.com); 51 Margaret Street (www.kissthehippo.com)

💬 **LOCAL SECRET**

Sometimes—just sometimes—the much-maligned TripAdvisor delivers total gold. Read any editorial list of "Chelsea's best restaurants" and *The Chelsea Corner* will appear in absolutely none; yet the giant review platform accords it top billing (and thirteenth overall in London) and a maximum score. Quite correctly, as it turns out: Italian classics from calamari fritti to penne arrabiata are cooked with quiet brilliance and use palpably fresh, quality ingredients. Helping things along further is the nice decor, brass and whites, plus lots of plants, and, unsurprisingly, a delectable tiramisu worth the trip alone.

451 Fulham Road (+44 20 3055 0088, www.thechelseacorner.com)

▲▶ UK Barista Champions in 2018 and 2019, all of Kiss The Hippo's coffees are roasted carbon-neutral in an energy efficient and environmentally friendly roaster.

South London

ENGLAND

> No part of the capital has more of an "us and them" mentality, with the chip on South Londoners' shoulders chiefly fueled by their domain being so permanently maligned by other Londoners. That includes food, and again, unfairly, there's far more "down south" than endless Morley's chicken takeaway restaurants or builders' caffs—you just need to know where to look.

ON A BUDGET?

Eight years ago, *The Observer's* food critic Jay Rayner journeyed to rough-and-ready Camberwell and ravely reviewed Turkish joint FM Mangal, alerting thousands to low-price yet top-notch kebabs. Last year, Rayner returned to the now-readier, less-rough district to pour acclaim on *Nandine*, a Kurdish joint serving shakshuka, slabs of spiced lamb, zingy capers, and fries coated in yogurt, pomegranate, and sesame seeds. The prices are just as bonkers low. *Mamma Dough's* six pizzerias—our favorite being the cozy Ladywell branch—aren't quite as cheap, but their sumptuous sourdough "Devil," laden with nduja and onions, still constitutes a bargain at a mere £11.

45 Camberwell Church Street (+44 20 8001 8322, www.nandine.co.uk);
40 Ladywell Road (+44 20 8690 7550, www.mammadough.co.uk)

SPLASH OUT

South London's grandest tables occupy its most recognizable building. Along with seasonal tasting menus, *Aqua Shard*—in, yes, The Shard—affords preposterous panoramic views from its 31st-floor perch. So, should conversation be lagging by dessert, there's ample distraction. Fine food and vistas, this time of Wandsworth Common, also await in Michelin-starred Chez Bruce, but for unstuffier surrounds try *Levan* in ever-foodier Peckham. While "bistronomy"-style sharing plates such as cuttlefish risotto or quince-mustard pork chops for £18.50 stretch wallets (less so the legendary comté fries, at £6.50), no one will fold your napkin when you visit the loo.

31 St. Thomas Street (+44 20 3011 1256, www.aquashard.co.uk); 12–16 Blenheim Grove (+44 20 7732 2256, www.levanlondon.co.uk)

PUB PERFECTION

The Canton Arms was rough once; then it became the ultimate gastropub. So, these days the punch-ups, druggies, and wee have been replaced by partridge, dauphinoise potatoes, and watercress. Good call. You'll also find ox-heart pastrami, plum fizz, pumpkin and sweetcorn croquettes, and the foie gras brioche toasties, which first earned this still-cozy Lambeth boozer its foodie fame. Though ambitious, the cooking is never arrogant. Decent roasts are served, too, as at Herne Hill's lovely The Florence, opposite Brockwell Lido, yet neither can match **The Gun's** right-on-the-river views over in Canary Wharf. Pigs in blankets and Yorkshire puddings accompany quality meats here every Sunday.

177 South Lambeth Road (+44 20 7582 8710, www.cantonarms.com); 27 Coldharbour (+44 20 7519 0075, www.thegundocklands.com)

LOCAL SECRET

Tooting's brouhaha hides some terrific independent eats. Take **Namak Mandi**, one of Britain's few restaurants devoted to Pashtun cuisine (from northwest Pakistan) and its sparse ingredients, soft spices, and fatty meats. Kabuli pulao, involving fronds of caramelized carrots and raisins atop an ultra-tender lamb shank, typifies the offerings. You sit on floor cushions and there's complimentary rice pudding, slow-cooked for eight hours, afterward. Much further east, Greenwich's plain-looking **Zaibatsu** does tremendous Japanese fusion food at a fraction of Central London rates. Everything—the dragon rolls, the peanut tofu, the eel sushi, the katsu curry, and the green tea ice cream—is absolutely scintillating.

▲ All of the tables at the Aqua Shard offer panaromic views of London—a feast for the eyes.

25 Upper Tooting Road (+44 20 8767 6120); 96 Trafalgar Road (+44 20 8858 9317, www.zaibatsufusion.co.uk)

REGIONAL FAVES

Brixton has boasted a strong Caribbean population ever since the first "Windrush generation" were housed nearby in 1948. Before it went all fancy foodie, its market retained a distinctly tropical flavor while up Brixton Road you'll still find a joyous Jamaican restaurant. **Negril** serves plenty of plantain and ackee, saltfish fritters, sweet potato fries, Rastafarian vegan stews, and curried goat. For all that, there's really only one order here: the free-range jerk chicken (or ribs, or burgers), bursting with zingy flavor. Smooth reggae plays all the while and prices are low. Expect to leave in a very good mood indeed.

132 Brixton Hill (+44 20 8674 8798, www.negrilonline.co.uk)

🍽 BRILL FOR BRUNCH

Replete with wealthy young families and anchored by its strollable common, Clapham makes an obvious brunch hotspot. Always busy—you can't reserve, so come early—is *Brew*, thanks largely to its diverse and distinct all-day menu. Sweetcorn fritters and pan-fried haloumi pide represent the savory end, with toasted banana bread rather naughtier, and treacle-cured bacon sandwiches somewhere in between. More standard granolas, pancakes, and egg

dishes are also present and correct, while breakfast martinis and Malteser milkshakes make for decadent beverages. If you can't get to Clapham, Brew also has branches in Wandsworth and tennis-mecca Wimbledon.

45 Northcote Road (+44 20 7585 2198, www.brew-cafe.com)

🍺 BEER OH BEER

It might be busy and a bit knobbish, but the Bermondsey Beer Mile does contain high-quality breweries. *Fourpure* has an especially long range of refreshments and its taproom opens six days a week—rare for London. New brewer Southey operates a taproom in Penge, where hipsters and betting-shop sluggards share streets, but nicer is its *London Beer Dispensary* in leafy Crofton Park. A sequel to Gipsy Hill's much-missed Beer Rebellion, this bar serves global guest ales and burgers despite lacking a physical bar. Taps instead line a wall, one you stand next to while knowledgeable staff pour and chat. Genius.

◀ You can't book a table at Brew, so make sure you arrive early to take advantage of their blissful blueberry pancakes.

Bermondsey Trading Estate, 22 Rotherhithe New Rd (+44 20 3744 2141, www.fourpure.com); 389 Brockley Road (+44 20 8694 6962, www.southeybrewing.co.uk)

🍸 KILLER COCKTAILS

While it's tricky to recommend *Louie Louie* for dinner given the café's rotating chefs-in-residence, its slick cocktail—and sometimes DJ—basement is more dependable. Dependably delicious is an Up All Night, consisting of tequila, cardamom-infused cold-brew coffee, coffee liqueur, and chocolate bitters. In riverside Putney, meanwhile, it's all about fun. Open-air in summer, *The Toy Shop* is liable to serve drinks in Lego-like cups you can keep, has a ping-pong table (Sun–Wed), and offers options such as Revenge of The Gingerbread Man (vodka, kumquats, lime, and gingerbread syrup), which comes with a free, homemade gingerbread man. I repeat: free gingerbread.

347 Walworth Road (+44 20 7450 3223, www.louielouie.london); 32 High Street (+44 20 8704 1188, www.thetoyshopbar.com)

 **CAFFEINE KICKS**

Before requesting a long black or latte in London Bridge's *Roasting Plant*, customers must first select a coffee blend. Just-roasted single-origin beans are then pressure fired through huge transparent pipes—think Willy Wonka's factory—to machines. Behind are lots of comfy, low-lit seats and an extravagantly high ceiling. Elsewhere, South London these days abounds with specialist, simpler coffee shops. One of the best is *Four Boroughs* in hilltop Crystal Palace. Its pared-back, pine interiors complement a fuss-free philosophy—assembly coffee (plus kombucha and craft beer), healthy snacks, artwork for sale, good music, and really friendly service.

4 Borough High Street (+44 20 7357 0405, www.roastingplant. co.uk); 10 Church Road (www. fourboroughs.co.uk)

MARKET RESEARCH

Food markets are South London's specialist subject. The headline act is busy *Borough Market*, a sprawling, under-the-train-tracks space, which somehow combines classic marketplace grime with culinary boundary crossing. Open daily are basic stalls, specialist venison burger or

▲ Borough Market continues to be one of London's best, with a whole host of flavorsome food on offer throughout the week.

ganache stands, and, above and around, a bevy of in-vogue restaurants ranging from pasta specialist Padella to taqueria El Pastor. Not quite two miles east, *Maltby Street Market* (Fri–Sun only) is calmer, much smaller, and more determinedly artisan. Along an alley by railway arches you'll find grilled cheese sandwiches, peanut butter brownies, and sourdough baguettes—yum!

(www.boroughmarket.org.uk); (www.maltby.st)

East London

ENGLAND

> Lots of foodie places in the City, Shoreditch, and co are no secret at all; figuring that you'll already know about them or won't have to work hard in order to do so, this section concentrates, by and large, on more secretive spots. That covers pease pudding in Poplar, vegan brunch in Homerton, and craft beer plus Colombian food in waterside Hackney Wick.

💰 ON A BUDGET?

Two cuisines dominate when it comes to cheap East London eats: curry (try Whitechapel's legendary *Tayyabs*) and Vietnamese (Hoxton's Cay Tre is great). But there are other options to explore. On Dalston's rough edged Ridley Road market, *Ararat Bread* will do you a delectable lamb mince-stuffed, sesame-topped hot Pakistani naan for a preposterous £2, while Brick Lane's *Beigel Bake*—open 24/7, and as busy at 1am as 1pm—sells boiled, Jewish-style bagels plumped with salt beef, salmon, cream cheese, or whatever you fancy from just 90p. No wonder it's an institution.

83–89 Fieldgate Street (+44 20 7247 9543, www.tayyabs.co.uk); 132 Ridley Rd (+44 75 8152 2418); 159 Brick Lane (+44 20 7729 0616, www.facebook.com/beigelbake)

PUB PERFECTION

The best thing about *The Royal Oak* isn't its corner location beside Columbia Road's photogenic Sunday flower market. Nor its cozy, laurel green interiors, or an appearance in *Lock, Stock and Two Smoking Barrels*. Nope, it's those yummy sausage rolls, delivered with spicy mustard, ketchup, or both. They. Are. Heaven. If you're a beer buff, however, steer your palate toward Old Street and *The Fountain*, which has been run by the same family for half a century. Nearly 20 craft ales are on tap, including offerings by London stalwarts Five Points and some funkier UK brands. Imbibe amid a nice terrace or admire, unexpectedly, the fish tank.

73 Columbia Road (+44 20 7729 2220, www.royaloaklondon.com); 3 Baldwin Street (+44 20 7253 2970, www.oldfountain.co.uk)

▼ The famous Beigel Bake always has a queue of people out the door desperate to get their hands on a salt beef bagel.

SPLASH OUT

Hawksmoor's Spitalfields outpost is now even more beautiful, thanks to new dark green leather banquettes and a clubby look. It remains one of London's premier beef specialists—along with Gaucho—as well as a seriously sensible choice for posh Sunday roasts, slow grilled on charcoal. By night, steak hounds are offered a choice of cuts, sauces (from Bearnaise to bone marrow gravy), and sides, then await their flame cooked

heaven. Another oldie and goodie is *St John*, in Smithfield market, where unpretentious staples, such as Welsh rarebit and deviled kidneys are done well enough to earn the restaurant a Michelin star, all amid a whitewashed ex-smokehouse.

157a Commercial Street (+44 20 7426 4850, www.thehawksmoor. com); 26 St John Street (+44 20 7251 0848, www.stjohnrestaurant. com)

BRILL FOR BRUNCH

If this book had a cookie category, *Esters* would be an automatic pick. You could lump this sharp little Stoke Newington square under coffee, too, thanks to atypical blends from Staffordshire roastery Has Bean. Instead, though, let's gush about the brunches. All of them, from French toast with fruit and ricotta, to Chinese spiced pork with a crispy fried egg and toast, are sensational. Two other places compare: modern Spitalfields restaurant *Crispin* for its sublime three cheese toasties with poached eggs, and *I Will Kill Again* in Homerton, the excellent name matched by Canadian beans with vegan chorizo served on shared tables.

55 Kynaston Rd (+44 20 7254 0253, www.estersn16.com); White's Row (+44 20 7247 1173, www.crispinlondon.com); 27a Ponsford Street (+44 20 3774 0131, www.instagram.com/ iwillkillagain)

▲ ▶ Spitafields was Hawsmoor's first restaurant and it truly captures the spirit of this celebrated steakhouse with great food, drinks, and atmosphere.

REGIONAL FAVES

The old East End— think Cockney rhyming slang and the Krays—is indelibly associated with two working-class dishes. One can be enjoyed at *BJ's Pie & Mash* in Canning Town (proper East London). Crammed with beef and rich gravy, its near-burnt pastries are accompanied by liquor (parsley sauce), creamy mash, and another classic, stewed eels. The second dish is pease pudding, a northern import involving boiled split yellow peas. *Ivy's* has served it, plus saveloys and faggot stuffing, for 60 years, although the café's Poplar home of Chrisp Street Market is being regenerated, and its future, sadly, is in serious doubt.

330 Barking Road (+44 20 7474 3389); Market Square (www. chrispstreet.com/item/ivys)

🍺 BEER OH BEER

First Hackney Wick had watermills, drawing on the River Lea and manufacturing crepe and rope. Then, when these became derelict, it has artist studios and raves. Now, more gentrified, it has craft beer—typified by *Crate*, a brewery whose canal side taproom serves its own mango sponsored pale plus guest ales from the likes of Old Chimney. There's outdoor seating if it's warm and a pizzeria and DJs some evenings. Indulge, indulge some more, and then relocate several steps to *Howling Hops'* attractive Tank Bar, where picnic table benches, distressed chequerboard floors, and Colombian food accompany the tipples.

▲ Pick a spot next to the River Lea to sample Crate's range of beers and stone-baked pizzas.

Unit 7 Queen's Yard, White Post Ln (+44 20 8533 3331, www. cratebrewery.com); Unit 9A Queen's Yard (+44 20 3583 8262, www.howlinghops.co.uk/tank-bar)

▲ Howling Hops started out drinking beer, then they sold it at The Southampton Arms (see *North London*, page 24), and now they're brewing it.

CAFFEINE KICKS

Specialist coffee abounds in the East these days, with a profusion of minimal, geek chic cafés. Ozone, Grind, Workshop and Taylor St are among the best purveyors, yet all well-documented, so let's laud three less-hailed spots. The first is in Shoreditch's iconic Tea Building. *Lyle's* is famed for its modern British restaurant, but the international coffee—sometimes starring Austria's sainted JB Kaffee—is just as admirable. Then there's *Lanark*, rotating roasters such as Alchemy and Dark Arts close to Hackney City Farm, and the pink themed *Palm Vaults* in Hackney itself, where vegan food, succulents, and multicolored lattes can improve even the worst days.

56 Shoreditch High Street (+44 20 3011 5911, www.lyleslondon. com); 262 Hackney Road (www. lanarkcoffee.co.uk); 411 Mare Street (www.palmvaults.com)

KILLER COCKTAILS

East of Shoreditch's increasing swish and still pleasingly neighborhood vibe, Bethnal Green has emerged as an unlikely cocktail hub in the past decade. The low-key Satan's Whiskers and railway arch-set *Sager & Wilde* merit visits, but French-inspired, exposed brick den *Coupette* is the standout as it allows for the combo of croque monsieurs with champagne piña coladas. No more needs to be said. Equally noteworthy is *Hacha* in Dalston: an

"agaveria" whose tequila and mezcal-championing owner deserves credit for such potions as the entirely transparent Mirror Margarita.

Arch 250 Paradise Row (+44 20 7729 6278, www.sagerandwilde. com/paradise-row); 423 Bethnal Green Road (+44 20 7729 9562, www.coupette.co.uk); 378 Kingsland Road (www.hachabar. com)

DATE FOR TWO

Duck & Waffle is one of those well-trodden places this guide can't avoid because, ultimately, there's nothing more romantic than a good view. Especially if it's from a 40th-floor perch in the City, and *especially* if said perch is open 24 hours and has ox cheek donuts with apricot jam on its menu. Closer to the ground yet rather wobblier is *Barge East*, a restored Dutch boat on the River Lea, back in Hackney Wick. Its short seasonal menu might yield lamb sweetbreads or bass in a creamy vermouth sauce; eat it outside, looking at the Olympic Stadium on balmy days, or otherwise inside near a log fire.

Heron Tower, 110 Bishopsgate

◀ Set in an old railway arch, Sager & Wilde is a bar and kitchen spotlighting cocktails, wines, and modern British fare.

▲ Duck & Waffle provide all-day dining from sunrise to sunset to sunrise again.

◀ Dine on 114-year-old Barge East, which sailed from Holland to Hackney Wick by three childhood friends.

(+44 20 3640 7310, www. duckandwaffle.com); Sweetwater Mooring, White Post Lane (+44 20 3026 2807, www.bargeeast.com)

MARKET RESEARCH

Two bustling street markets for your money here. Containing the revered Climpson & Sons coffee shop, Banh Mi baguettes, brownies, burgers, hipsters, hagglers, and buskers galore, foodie *Broadway Market* (Saturdays only) is jam-packed joy, even if it is impossible to move. Once you do finally escape, there are good places to sit: Regent's Canal at one end, London Fields opposite. To the north, in Clapton, the edgy place Dalston once was, is the *Chatsworth Road Market* (Sundays only), which hosted Alan Sugar's first sale—of shampoo, if you're wondering. Leading the culinary offering are Le Moulin's fruitcakes and Greek kebabs from Souvlaki Street.

www.broadwaymarket.co.uk; www.chatsworthroade5.co.uk/market

Whitstable, Margate,

and surrounding areas

ENGLAND

> The northern and eastern stretches of Kent's coast are dotted by rebooted towns: most famously Margate, dainty Deal, bivalve-obsessed Whitstable, arty Folkestone, and even Charles Dickens' regal old haunt Broadstairs. All of which leads to a beguiling mix of trendy, hipster, and inventive cocktails alongside legendary beach pubs and centuries-old oyster bars.

ON A BUDGET?

GB Pizza Co began life as a pop-up, with Rachel and Lisa traveling around Britain—hence the name—in a vintage Volkswagen campervan. Having been smitten by Margate, they now have a cheery seafront home in the town's trendiest, most revived area, off the Parade. And despite repeated acclaim—one *Telegraph* reviewer pronounced it the best pizza she'd ever had—prices remain low. Uniformly cooked in a wood-fired oven, a Margate-rita (get it?) costs £6.50, while a wackier pear and blue cheese is £9. Even cheaper is Dover's *Happy Chef*, a smart looking greasy spoon that delivers superior cooking, stellar service, and castle views.

14 Marine Drive (+44 1843 297700, www.greatbritishpizza. com); 131–132 Snargate Street (+44 1304 448259, www.facebook.com/ thehappychefdover)

 SPLASH OUT

The Sportsman is the sole Kent coast establishment to boast a Michelin star, and has repeatedly been named national gastropub of the year. Found on a far-flung beach road west of Whitstable, it's a white inn that uses Thames estuary fish and Kentish meat

▲ Holding a Michelin star since 2008, The Sportsman takes inspiration for its dishes from its surroundings, serving fresh fish from the North Sea and meat and vegetables from the marshland, woods, and soil.

◀ A former pub, The Rose is a seaside bar, restaurant, and hotel that serves seriously good food.

for palpably simple—roast chicken with sausage and truffle cream sauce, for example—à la carte and tasting menus. Further south in pretty Deal, where Georgian terraces abut fishermen's cottages, newly trendy hotel *The Rose's* food is overseen from afar by Polpo alumna Rachel O'Sullivan. It's as fun—

mussels spunked up by 'nduja and saffron, or grilled cheesy courgettes—as the wall-mounted Tracey Emin.

Faversham Road, near Seasalter (+44 1227 273370, www. thesportsmanseasalter.co.uk); 91 High Street (+44 1304 389127, www.therosedeal.com/restaurant)

REGIONAL FAVES

Whitstable, of course, is most famous for its Native oysters: large, succulent bivalves that The Whitstable Oyster Company reckons to have been farming for 600 years. If you can't make July's annual festival, do the next best thing and visit **Wheelers Oyster Bar**, the town's oldest restaurant. A four-stool shop—that also offers crab sandwiches and quiche for takeaway—gives way to an only slightly bigger parlor room serving three course dinners amid mounted plates and framed pictures. Reservations are essential given the small size, and you can book two months ahead.

8 High Street (+44 1227 273311, www.wheelersoysterbar.com)

▲ Book in advance and bring your own booze to Wheelers Oyster Bar, Whitstable's oldest and much-loved restaurant.

DATE FOR TWO

When he opened **Rocksalt**—plus posh chippie The Smokehouse—ex-Claridge's cook Mark Sargeant spearheaded Folkestone's subsequent regeneration, one which has also wrought an art-depositing triennial. Now accompanied by four bedrooms, Rocksalt's fuss-free Dover sole or black pudding dishes remain superb, while its floor-to-ceiling harbor views are deeply romantic. No less intimate is **Stark**, an ex-sandwich bar in perpetually charming Broadstairs run by the very talented (and very tattooed) Ben Crittenden. In his 12-seat space, there is but one option: a daring six-course tasting menu,

▼ Another Michelin-starred restaurant on the Kent coast is Stark, an intimate and relaxed setting serving great quality food.

which might include pressed pork, peach, gooseberry, gurnard, or all four.

4-5 Fishmarket (+44 1303 212070, www.rocksaltfolkestone. co.uk); 1 Oscar Road (www. starkfood.co.uk)

🍰 TIME FOR TEA

Inspired by Lewis Carroll's famous story—"Take some more tea," the March Hare said to Alice—*Alice and the Hatter* is an appropriately bonkers Herne Bay hidey-hole of throne chairs, teacup stools, love seats, and grassy nooks. Children are made very welcome, and the myriad, calorific afternoon options incorporate homemade cakes, toasted teacakes, and "scioches"—scone and brioche fusions—all served on themed crockery. High tea must be booked 24 hours in advance; otherwise, just show up and prepare to have a lot of fun. To paraphrase the Cheshire Cat, "they're all mad there."

24 William Street (+44 1227 467937, www.aliceandthehatter. co.uk)

💬 LOCAL SECRET

Typifying Margate's artsy, indie temperament, *Hantverk & Found* is both a commissioning art gallery (Thurs–Sun) and soulful

▲ A welcome addition to Dover's high street, The Allotment's menus change with the seasons (and market supply).

seafood bistro whose menus are chalk-written on a buffed out black wall. The art, mainly watercolors, is by local talents, while the bistro is defined by what's available. There's a Japanese influence behind miso-marinated mackerel fillets with sesame sauce and kimchi, while bream fillets plus celeriac and potato purée are pure fall. Local sourcing informs *The*

Allotment in Dover, too: much of its produce comes from private gardeners around town. Dishes aren't particularly innovative, but their cooking explains a loyal following.

16-18 King Street (+44 1843 280454, www.hantverk-found.co. uk); 9 High Street (+44 1304 214467, www. theallotmentrestaurant.com)

PUB PERFECTION

"Cavalry saddles, pieces of barbozettes, firkins of butter." So reads a sign in the **Ship Inn**, advertising the spoils of an 1817 wreck and epitomizing the nautical curios adorning this dim, trapped-in-time Deal boozer. Handpumps dispense Dark Star and Ramsgate concoctions, while a garden awaits behind. Down the coast, past Edwardian villas and colorful beach huts, stands Kingsdown's **The Zetland Arms**, one of Kent's many dreamily positioned seaside pubs. Families come here after a paddle on the adjacent shingle, lured by seafood chowders and burgers, or perhaps simply a Shepherd Neame ale. On a sunny day you can see as far as France.

141 Middle Street (+44 1304 372222); Wellington Parade (+44 1304 370114, www.zetlandarms.co.uk)

▲ A hole-in-the-wall café, Mala Kaffe brings a taste of Swedish *fika* culture to Margate.

▼ With a prime location on the beaches of Deal, and offering stunning sea views, The Zetland Arms is the perfect place to enjoy a drink at sundown.

CAFFEINE KICKS

In Folkestone's Creative Quarter, near studios and enticing stores, is **Steep Street Coffee House**, a bookshop café from the local coffee roasters. Sipping espressos and lattes that utilize Store Street's own globally sourced beans, visitors can peruse fiction titles or hardback tomes in the tradition of early Parisian coffee spaces. Homemade sweets and savories are also available. If Paris inspires that, Swedish culture—and owners—are behind Margate's **Mala Kaffe**. The social coffee and cake tradition of *fika* lives on here, courtesy of cardamom buns and Allpress grind. Better still, a position at the end of the Harbour Arm ensures fine sea views and gorgeous sunsets.

18–24 The Old High Street (+44 1303 247819, www. steepstreet.co.uk); Unit 3, Harbour Arm (+44 7375 534867, www.facebook.com/malakaffe)

BRILL FOR BRUNCH

Pleasure piers and good eats rarely go hand in hand, but Deal's award-winning tentacle breaks the mould. Newly instaled at its end is the **Deal Pier Kitchen**, using local, organic food for an all-day brunch menu scoffed amid slatted wooden ceilings and turquoise tiles. The classics— sweetcorn fritters, shakshuka, smashed avo—are accompanied by vegan options and unusual contenders like soft-boiled eggs with cheesy soldiers. There's also a Booze

▶ Laying claim to another outstanding location, Deal Pier Kitchen sits at the very end of the town's jetty, offering sea views for miles as well as the promise of great food and even better coffee.

Brunch option if you're feeling reckless. A shout out, too, to **Samphire** in Whitstable, whose salt beef hashes with fried duck eggs and avocado plus fermented chili on toast are available until 5pm.

Deal Pier (www.facebook.com/ dealpierkitchen), 4 High Street (+44 1227 770075, www.samphirewhitstable.co.uk)

KILLER COCKTAILS

Will Ramsgate be the next Kent town to go cool? If so, places like **Zest** will help. A café and cocktail bar combined, it's fresh in every way: fresh ingredients, fresh owners in young couple Tyler and Chris, and, courtesy of the latter, fresh mixology ideas picked up during time spent in Norway. Witness his cherry and coconut sour, jalapeño martini, or Chai Life, starring rum, vanilla chai, and aperol. All feature handmade syrups. If you're feeling peckish, Tyler, who has worked under Marco Pierre White in Dubai, can prepare vegan pulled pork or her Instagram Burger, involving a black charcoal bun.

18 Queen Street (+44 1843 586920, www.facebook.com/ zestcafeandbar)

Brighton, Eastbourne, Hastings,

and surrounding areas

ENGLAND

> Between them, the three resort towns of Brighton, Eastbourne, and Hastings have more or less everything covered. Daring fine dining? Check. Incredible ice cream? Check. Specialty coffee, craft beer, and bravura brunches? Check, check, and check. All that's lacking are some award-winning vineyards and irresistible delicatessens—but don't worry, these are hiding just inland.

ON A BUDGET?

Elegant Eastbourne has seen a clump of independent restaurants open on Terminus Road and in its Little Chelsea area of late, yet none rival the family run **Dolphin Fish Bar** for value. High-quality, fresh-off-the-boat cod, plaice, haddock, huss (dogfish), and skate with crispy chips start from £6.30, and there's a sit-down restaurant. Consider also **Judges Bakery** and its legendary "mack-a-rolls," filled with smoked mackerel. If you're in Brighton, the vegetarian **Planet India's** prices—£7.81 for a spinach and paneer curry, for instance—are pleasingly peculiar and, given the quality on offer, pleasingly low.

86 Seaside (+44 1323 722813, www.dolphinfishbar.com); 51 High Street (+44 1424 722588, www.judgesbakery.com); 4 Richmond Parade (+44 1273 818149, www.planetindia.co.uk/brighton)

SPLASH OUT

This coastline's glammest residence is Eastbourne's whitewashed Grand Hotel, and such five-star finery has an appropriately classy, ambitious restaurant. **The Mirabelle's** head chef Stephanie Malvoisin, lured from the Laura Ashley Manor hotel, plays with European classics for tasting-menu treats like goats' cheese cannelloni or seared quail breasts with beetroot purée. At **The Salt Room**, an attractive exposed brick room facing Brighton's West Pier, thrilling seafood plates—slow-cooked salmon with yuzu and salt-baked bream whose crust waiters will prize open—segue into the "Taste of the Pier" dessert sharing board, starring such Instagrammable wonders as strawberry and lime donuts and mincemeat 99 flakes.

King Edward's Parade (+44 1323 412345, www.grand eastbourne.com/mirabelle-restaurant); 106 King's Rd (+44 1273 929488, www.saltroom-restaurant.co.uk)

ICE-CREAM DREAM

Athletes always need refueling so, after an epic round on Hastings' crazy golf course, retreat a few steps to *Di Polas* and tuck into generous scoops of ice cream—available in flavors from sticky toffee and custard to Nutella—while reviewing that windmill hole. Should hydration urgently be required, order a milkshake. Further west, Brighton's bulging dessert scene is headlined by **Boho Gelato**, where Italian-trained owner Seb oversees more daring flavors. Four hundred of them, in fact,

with 24 available daily: vegan Creme Egg is a bestseller, while sour cherry delights classicists. Of their two shops, the seaside Pool Valley branch has lots more seating.

14 Marine Parade (+44 1424 203666, www.facebook.com/dipolas); 6 Pool Valley (+44 1273 727205, www.bohogelato.co.uk)

BRILL FOR BRUNCH

Brunch in Brighton's Lanes is a lovely experience, especially if you can snaffle a window seat and watch the hungover world troop by. So, step forward **Lost In The Lanes**, where an all-day brunch menu, ranging from avocado and salmon on sourdough to orange

▲ Boho Gelato handmakes over 400 flavors of Italian-style ice cream, including vegan and gluten-free varieties.

▲ An independent coffee shop, Nelson Coffee serves exceptional coffee, loose-leaf tea, and delicious food to boot.

and Earl Grey granola, is served alongside smoothies and cappuccinos in stripped-back surrounds. Go early to beat the inevitable queue. Opposite the station in Eastbourne, **Nelson Coffee** sources artisan everything: java, loose-leaf tea, Toulouse sausages, haloumi, and so on. Its brunch options include veggie fritter stacks, three cheese toasties, and mushroom and 'nduja omelettes.

10 Nile Street (+44 1273 525444, www.lostinthelanes.com); 4 Terminus Road (www.nelsoncoffee.co.uk)

DATE FOR TWO

Chiefly renowned for its raucous Bonfire Night celebrations, the medieval market town of Lewes also has beckoning boutiques and *Limetree Kitchen*, an indie restaurant devoted to minimal waste and a use it all "nose to tail" philosophy around ingredients. Its intimate room of white wooden boards and simple tables feels romantic, as do shareable portions of cauliflower pakoras or crispy pig's head. Couples in Brighton are directed to *Mediterraneo*, a dinky Sicilian den speckled with candlelight, two person tables, red rugs, and erotic paintings. Order traditional lasagne or limoncello torte, and make sure to reserve well in advance: they only open for dinner on Fridays and Saturdays.

14 Station Street (+44 1273 478636, www.limetreekitchen.co.uk); 164 Portland Road (www.mediterraneorestaurants.co.uk)

BEER OH BEER

A microbrewery at *The First In Last Out* sees this Hastings pub produce six regular ales, among them the chocolate malt Mike's Mild. You'll also find booths, backgammon, and a back room where diners can scoff corned beef hash or Bramley apple and

▲ The Rathfinny Estate is renowned for its award-winning wines, but their Tasting Room restaurant gives visitors the opportunity to enjoy small bites, lunch, and dinner, too.

berry crumble, but no jukeboxes or televisions showing sport. As for Brighton, there are some 60 local breweries, headlined by the award winning Darkstar, and thus lots of craft beer pubs for their probably bearded partakers. Try *Idle Hands*, not only for its ten taps devoted to artisan British ales, but for its dim Victorian setting and regular jazz shows.

14–15 High Street (+44 1424 425079, www.thefilo.co.uk); 59 Queens Road (+44 1273 770760, www.idlehandsbrighton.com)

PERPETUAL WINE

Vineyards in Sussex and Kent are producing award-winning sparkling wines, which reliably best French champagne houses at competition level. One such is the vast *Rathfinny* estate, beside the South Downs near Alfriston, where Michelin acclaimed eats are accompanied by regular tours and a cellar tasting room. Otherwise, head for St Leonards, a town beside Hastings dubbed "Dalston on Sea" for its newfound cool vibe. Plonk knowledge abounds at oenophile bars Graze on Grand (also an excellent restaurant) and atmospheric *Farmyard*, in which platters of local charcuterie and cheeses complement a biodynamic glass of sauvignon blanc, beaujolais, nero d'avola, or catarratto.

White Way (+44 1323 871031, www.rathfinnyestate.com); 52 Kings Road (+44 1424 420020, www.farmyardwine.com)

SUITCASE SWAG

Still, if you really want to taste regional *fromage*, Hastings has an even better option. The bijou and utterly lovely *Penbuckles Delicatessen* stocks Sussex bries and Tunworth camembert among 50 cheeses, as well as regional chutneys and organic wines. (In Lewes, Cheese Please has a similarly good range—and holds tastings.) To the north in Battle, 1066 devotees visiting the partially ruined abbey should skip its gift shop in favor of the *Battle Deli & Coffee Shop*, which stocks all the gingerbread, damson jam, tea, palmiers, and anchovies you'll ever need—and serves yummy cake to boot.

50 High Street (+44 1424 465050, www.facebook.com/penbuckles); 78 High Street (+44 1424 777810, www.facebook.com/battledeli)

TEA TIME

Even closer to Battle Abbey—on whose ground the Battle of Hastings, despite its name, was fought, don't you know—stands *Mrs Burton's*, founded on the eternal verity that tourists will always need tea. Catering to lactose, gluten, and savory intolerants alike, this is a traditional place of embroidered tablecloths and fine china, of toasted teacakes, and—oh yes—sherry trifle. Matching principles underpin *The Cobbles Tea Room* in Rye, an artsy Cinque Port settlement that might be just Sussex's handsomest town amid stellar competition. Cobbles majors in high-grade global teas and homemade hot scones plus jam and cream.

2 High Street (+44 1424 774204, www.mrsburtons.co.uk); 1 Hylands Yard (+44 7801 847687, www. facebook.com/thecobblesrye)

CAFFEINE KICKS

Brighton's sea of relocated London millennials means that Starbucks and co are never an option, explaining the city's legion of third wave coffee houses. Among a zillion good shouts, *Bond St. Coffee* stands out for utilizing single origin beans lightly manipulated at its own local-ish roastery, with two daily options, plus a whizzy La Marzocco espresso machine. And for their decadent sofas and latte art. Back in Lennies— as many locals call St Leonards—*Fika@44* has a bright, light Scandi style and a rear courtyard in which to enjoy its Alchemy coffee, perhaps with some ginger tiffin or espresso banana cake.

15 Bond Street (+44 1273 731300, www.bondstcoffee.co.uk); 44 Kings Road (+44 1424 552424, www.facebook.com/fikacoffee44)

▲ Battle Deli & Coffee Shop serves lovely lunches, homemade cakes, bakes, and salads.

Lyndhurst
and surrounding areas
ENGLAND

> The vogue for championing local produce reaches fever pitch in the New Forest thanks chiefly to a happy abundance of everything from mushrooms to Britain's take on *jamón ibérico*. And whether your days are spent admiring Beaulieu Abbey, taking foraging tours, pony-spotting, or gently biking across heathland, stellar food and drink is a vital part of the experience.

💲 ON A BUDGET?

Cafe Parisien is the sort of place that restores your faith. A French-run café in the central village-town of Lyndhurst, it has smile-happy owners, welcomes dogs, and serves unpretentious but very well done dishes. There are omelettes, jacket potatoes, baguettes—brie and grape, prawn—or spicy avocado and bacon paninis, all mostly under a fiver, and there's good coffee as well. If it's sunny, hope for space in the small back garden. A few doors down the High Street awaits another option for the cost-conscious, fish and chip shop *Bertie's*, whose excellent staples are also available for scoffing in a welcoming restaurant area.

64 High Street (+44 23 8028 4546); 36 High Street (+44 23 8028 4774, www.berties-of-lyndhurst.co.uk)

PUB PERFECTION

Seeking nowt but a pint and a pork pie? Then you'll be happiest at the thatched *Royal Oak* in Fritham, north of the A31. Over 400 years old, it serves the aforementioned plus Ploughmans and pickles for lunch (plus, sometimes, homemade chutneys and an unusual garlic and nettle cheese), amid three low-beamed bars. One has a log fire, while warmer days can be spent in a delightful garden with far-reaching rural views. Dogs are welcome, too. Chuck in real ales and homebrewed cider, and this is surely free house heaven, especially during or after a hike—which makes it handy that the Fritham Loop starts here.

SO43 7HJ (+44 23 8081 2606, www.royaloakfritham.co.uk

BEST FEST

Smoked & Uncut is a food and music festival held on three summer Saturdays at three hotels (non-guests are welcome)—two of which are in the New Forest: The Pig at Brockenhurst and luxurious Lime Wood. It attracts bigger names each time, with 2019 seeing the Kaiser Chiefs and Sister Sledge both play a date. Each bill also features DJs—previously Professor Green—and high-quality food stands, including a pop-up kitchen by Angela Hartnett (see *Splash Out*), plus a glamping village. If you'd rather just nosh, November's **New Forest**

Food & Drink Fortnight delivers woodland feasts and special tasting menus.

www.smokedanduncut.com; www.thenewforest.co.uk/food-and-drink

SUITCASE SWAG

Artisan nosh can be taken home from the Farmers' Market in Ringwood—to the Forest's west—held from 10am–2pm on the last Saturday of every month (and the penultimate in December). Buffalo mozzarella, pickles, pies, and fresh apple juice should all be available. Also tempting taste buds is Lyndhurst's **The Forage**

Deli & Eatery, thanks to wares spanning deli oak-aged gins, kombucha vinegar, and cheesy biscotti. If you're keener on wine, head south to **Setley Ridge** vineyard for tours and tastings, plus a farm shop where you can pick up bottles of their still or sparkling wine.

39 High Street (+44 23 8028 2396, www.facebook.com/theforagelyndhurst); Lymington Road (+44 1590 622246, www.setleyridge.co.uk)

ON THE TRAIL

Numerous New Forest food trails await for those who like to earn their gluttony via exercise. Clocking in at 25 miles, the bicycle-based **Woodland Wander** passes cider and fudge purveyors and stops for lunch near Arthur Conan Doyle's gravestone. Cyclists can also tackle the seven-mile **South Food Trail** from Brockenhurst to Burley along a disused train line, possibly with a cream tea pit stop at the Old Station Tea Rooms (see *Tea Time*), while walkers after an easy amble are directed to the 2.2-mile **Beaulieu Food Trail**, which loosely shadows the Beaulieu River enroute to the shipbuilding village Bucklers Hard.

www.thenewforest.co.uk

▼ New Forest Food & Drink Fortnight is an annual celebration of all the delicious local food and drink the region has to offer.

SPLASH OUT

Beaulieu's *Terrace Restaurant*, inside the ivy-swathed Montagu Arms hotel, has suffered two tough losses in recent years: that of its Michelin star after a 2016 refurbishment and then of raved-about cook Matthew Tomkinson. No matter. New head chef Matthew Whitfield has impressively been lured from New York's three-star Eleven Madison Park and promises modern British brilliance as he seeks to rewoo Michelin's judges. Another culinary A-lister in these parts is Angela Hartnett, who co-runs Lime Wood's laid-back *Hartnett Holder & Co* (and the accompanying cookery school), using local saddleback pork or just-smoked cod's roe for zesty Italian small plates.

▲ Hartnett Holder & Co is a relaxed and stylish restaurant whose menus full of Italian-influenced dishes change with the seasons.

Palace Lane (+44 1590 612324, www.montaguarmshotel.co.uk); Beaulieu Road (+44 23 8028 7177, www.limewoodhotel.co.uk/food/hh-and-co)

BRILL FOR BRUNCH

Laura, Ben, Tom, and Sam might sound like a pop band, but they're actually the friendly founders of *Frampton's*, an all-day Ringwood bar-restaurant, which excels at brunch. Signature dishes include pork belly, poached egg, and hollandaise atop a wholemeal crumpet, and sweet potato hash with optional chorizo. Prices reflect the quality ingredients: nice sourdough, proper butter, and so on. The coffee is good, too—strong, bitter, and blessed relief for third-wave obsessives who rarely leave London. If it's warm, there's outside seating; otherwise stay inside the former general store, some of its peeling walls left untouched in the name of shabby chic.

48–50 High Street (+44 1425 473114, www.framptonsbar.co.uk)

DATE FOR TWO

Confession: being located on the cobbled quayside in Lymington, facing the handsome Georgian town's titular river, means the *Elderflower* sits just outside of the New Forest. Still, the innovative British-French creations of high-caliber chef Andrew Du Bourg are well worth leaving the national park for. Solent sea bass hooked nearby and not long ago comes with plankton mayonnaise, and asparagus is cooked various ways alongside a soft-boiled gull's egg. Candles and corner tables scream romance. **The Pig** is another shout for lovers, not just because of its plant-festooned restaurant, but also the fireside lounges, home-from-home vibe, and bathtub-happy bedrooms.

4A Quay Street (+44 1590 676908, www.elderflowerrestaurant.co.uk); Beaulieu Road (+44 3452 259494, www.thepighotel.com/ brockenhurst)

TEA TIME

With its train station, traffic, and sports cars, chichi Brockenhurst feels like the New Forest's nucleus. It's exactly the sort of twee place which has a tearoom—and it has a very good one. *Rosie Lea*, also a bakery, serves just-cooked scones with optional clotted cream, jam, or savory yeast spread (really?) alongside a variety of cakes and cha. Local ingredients and vintage china are the norm. Lyndhurst's Acres Down Farm holds similar charm, while *The Old Station Tea Rooms* utilizes a vacant railway halt.

▼ This café starts its day on coffee and ends with beers, wines, and cocktails.

Savory—using cheddar and chive scones—and cream teas are available, as are toasted teacakes.

76 Brookley Road (+44 1590 622797, www.rosielea.co.uk); Station Road, Holmsley (+44 1425 402468, www.stationhouseholmsley.com)

BEER OH BEER

The Forest's fringes are home to various beer makers, from ale artisans to craft microbreweries. One of the latter is *Vibrant Forest*, whose headquarters on a small estate outside Hardley, east of Beaulieu, include a taproom and shop (Fri–Sun, afternoons only) where flavor-packed porters, ales, and sours such as the blueberry and blackcurrant-tinged Aurelia are available—always in dynamically designed cans or bottles. Right across the Forest, the more famous *Ringwood Brewery* produces popular ales like Boondoggle and Razor Back. Ninety-minute tours conclude in a tasting session, or you can just visit the store to stock up.

Unit 3 The Purlieu Centre, Hardley Industrial Estate (+44 23 8200 2200, www.vibrantforest.co.uk); 138 Christchurch Road (+44 1425 470303, www.ringwoodbrewery.co.uk)

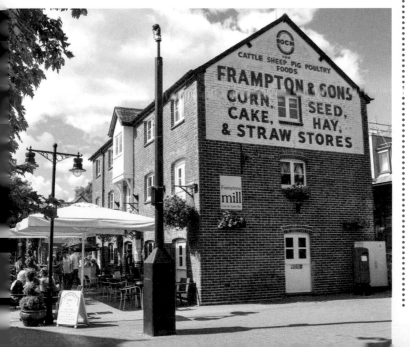

Padstow, Port Isaac,

and surrounding areas

ENGLAND

> **Messrs Stein, Ainsworth, and Outlaw are the culinary kingpins around these parts, each boasting their own empire of establishments along the pretty, surf-tastic coast. Yet dig deeper and you'll find plenty of other reasons to take your stomach westward, from farm shops and funked up off-licenses, to Du Maurier inns, Doom Bar pubs, and delectable tea rooms.**

and so on. Those rave reviews chiefly laud terrific service, huge portions, an accent on local produce and, yes, absurdly low prices. Further up coast in Port Isaac, where TV series *Doc Martin* is filmed, ***Nicky B's Pasty Shop*** on the harborside high street sells affordable, award-winning Cornish Pasties as well as sausage rolls.

South Quay (+44 7851 604350, www.facebook.com/benscribboxcafe); 22 Fore Street (+ 44 1208 880099)

💰 **ON A BUDGET?**
In Padstow you'll find establishments by super chefs Rick Stein and Paul Ainsworth—and yet the town's TripAdvisor restaurant rankings are topped by ***Ben's Crib Box Cafe***. A pine wood rectangle right on the quay, it serves everything a caff should: cooked breakfasts, burgers, cheesy chips, jacket potatoes,

SPLASH OUT

North Cornwall's other haloed kitchen wizard is Stein's former protege, Nathan Outlaw. And among the trio's flagship restaurants, it's *Restaurant Nathan Outlaw*—also in Port Isaac, but this time atop the hill, with rugged sea views—that, by fractions, most excites. Cornwall's first ever two Michelin star haunt, it serves an elite, sustainable seafood tasting menu full of sumptuous combinations and incredibly zingy flavors. Inland, *St Tudy's Inn* is a seventeenth-century village pub with four nice bedrooms where *Great British Menu* star Emily Scott manipulates the best Cornish fodder into homelier seasonal plates: think baked figs alongside honey, thyme, and ticklemore goats' cheese.

6 New Road (+44 1208 880896, www.nathan-outlaw.com/ restaurants); Chapel Lane (+44 1208 850656, www.sttudyinn. com)

PUB PERFECTION

As well as his various Padstow restaurants— explaining the town's "Padstein" moniker—Stein oversees another village boozer several miles west, the *Cornish Arms* in St Merryn. Thankfully, he has made few changes, concentrating on the kitchen. The net result is a proper pub (think pool tables and Sarson's vinegar bottles), which serves unusually good food at very reasonable prices. That fodder spans sausages and mash, real beef burgers, moules frites, and crab salads. As it's licensed by the St Austell Brewery, the den also has Tribute and Proper Job on tap to rival a long wine list.

On B3276, St Merryn (+44 1841 532700, www.rickstein.com/ the-cornish-arms.html)

BRILL FOR BRUNCH

Ideal before explorations of Tintagel Castle—a mystical island fortress where King Arthur was supposedly born—*Charlie's* lies in the village itself. As well as standards such as eggs benedict or pancake stacks under maple syrup, there's cinnamon and raisin toast with spiced pumpkin jam, and organic porridge enlivened by local clotted cream and honey. In Launceston, which has a ruined castle, stylish *No.8 Café & Delicatessen* does Big Cornish Breakfasts and smashed avocado on toast. Otherwise, retreat to the Aussie run Bush Pepper if you're in Newquay, while Padstow's best place for brunch is seaside Cherry Trees.

Fore Street (+44 1840 779500, www.charlies.cafe); Westgate Street (+44 1566 777369, www. no8launceston.co.uk)

▼ Owned by Rick Stein, The Cornish Arms offers a simple British pub menu alongside a great selection of ales, beers, and wine.

💬 LOCAL SECRET

Ainsworth's empire, meanwhile, extends to **Caffe Rojano**. Until recently, this was Rojano's on the Square, a trattoria where—as tourists flocked to the chef's Michelin-starred No 6—locals gobbled pizza or proper carbonara. Likely to be just as popular, its new iteration is an all-day New York-style Italian diner serving everything from slow cooked meatball marina to hot dogs topped under truffly mac and cheese. Southeast of Launceston, **Coombeshead Farm** is better known than once was (and you must reserve), but an inland location and faulty supposition that it's solely a B&B still deters many. Pitt Cue pioneer Tom Adams and April Bloomfield, from New York's Spotted Pig, perform magic with ingredients that are high quality, healthy, and much loved.

9 Mill Square (+44 1841 532093, www.paul-ainsworth.co.uk); Near Lewannick (www. coombesheadfarm.co.uk)

◀ Coombeshead is a farm, guesthouse, restaurant, and bakery.

▼ The Mariners champions the best of local produce to create classic British dishes.

🍺 BEER OH BEER

Cornwall's most popular ale, however, and indeed the UK's bestselling cask ale, is Doom Bar, made at **Sharp's Brewery** outside Rock, a fishing village across the River Camel from Padstow, and named after a local sand spit. The HQ itself has a visitor center and shop, with tastings available—ring for the latest—while the nearby pub, **The Mariners** (where Sharp's run the drinks offering), was relaunched last year by that same Paul Ainsworth, who took over from Outlaw. Overlooking the Camel Estuary on Rock's slipway, it pairs pints of Doom Bar with cream teas and classic British dishes.

Pityme Business Centre (+44 1208 862121, www.sharpsbrewery.co. uk); Slipway (+44 1841 532093, www.paul-ainsworth.co.uk)

☕ CAFFEINE KICKS

Cornwall's northernmost town, Bude, was a popular Victorian seaside resort and is today a surfing hotspot. Also, there is the remarkable **North Coast Wine Co**. Oliver Tullett took over a decrepit off-license in 2009; fast-forward a decade and the shelves bulge with 600 wines, plus spirits, ales, and ciders. Not only that, but there are 1930s cinema seats in which to enjoy some of those and, during daytimes, single-origin coffee from local roasters Sabins. Beans from a higher profile Cornish roastery, Origin, are used at Newquay's *Box & Barber Coffeehouse*, a surf-influenced shop, which is wholly biodegradable and dog friendly!

1 Lansdown Road (+44 1288 354304, www.ncwine.co.uk); 82 Fore Street (+44 7590 008007, www.facebook.com/boxandbarber)

SUITCASE SWAG

Just outside the eponymous village, which is partly, dramatically strung along a narrow inlet north of Tintagel, Penally Hill's *Boscastle Farm Shop* sells homemade pies and quiches as well as jars of jam, chutney, and pickled onions on bulging shelves. There's also a café serving afternoon teas and cottages in which to stay. You'll find a similar array of treats at the *Hilltop Farm Shop* in Slaughter Bridge, close to the River Camel, plus chocolates, cheeses, and even Christmas puddings. It too has a licensed café, a good place to rest after visiting the hamlet's Arthurian Centre.

Hillsborough Farm (+44 1840 250827, www.boscastlefarmshop. co.uk); Hilltop Farm (+44 1840 211518, www.facebook.com/ hilltopfarmshopcornwall)

DATE FOR TWO

Written into literary history by Daphne du Maurier's spooky novel of the same name and later adapted by Alfred Hitchcock, the *Jamaica Inn* is in Bolventor, a village in the center of Bodmin Moor. Though its walls also house a smuggling museum and food shop, the highlight is fireside dining in such a memorable spot—"murky dim in the darkness" as Du Maurier's heroine Mary Yellan arrives—with chicken and lemongrass pies and moussakas made from eggplant (aubergine) and zucchini (courgette) pepper accompanying pub classics. The "cold, dead atmosphere" encountered by Mary has, these days, been replaced by something a lot more welcoming.

Bolventor, off A30 (+44 1566 86250, www.jamaicainn.co.uk)

TEA TIME

Crantock, an ancient settlement across the River Gannel—ferries operate—from Newquay, is best known for its golden sand beach, and rightly so. But there's another reason to visit. Well, three, actually: freshly baked scones, Cornish clotted cream, and fine strawberry jam. This calorific holy trinity are offered at the summer only *Cosy Nook Tea Garden*, which also

▲ Made famous by Daphne du Maurier's story of the same name, the Jamaica Inn incorporates an inn, restaurant, bar, shop, and museum.

features a small gallery exhibiting and selling paintings, photography, and driftwood art. To the north, atop the jagged Bedruthan Steps, the *Carnewas Tearooms* majors in the same cream tea combos and slabs of cake. Its garden gloriously faces the Atlantic, offering great views.

Langurroc Road (+44 1637 830324, www.cosynookcrantock. co.uk); Bedruthan Steps, off B3276 (+44 1637 860701, www. carnewas-tea-rooms.co.uk)

Bath

ENGLAND

> Bath is only small, but it can still be hard work getting around this compact city—there are hills and crowds aplenty—meaning you'll need good fodder to keep you going. Happily, the Georgian honeypot has it covered. From a country-leading vegan scene through afternoon teas and orgasmic jam, to cocktail bars with a West Country slant, the food and drink scene here is reason enough to visit in its own right.

💲 ON A BUDGET?

While Bath is a tourist trap that knows it's pretty—resulting in higher than normal tariffs—the city also arguably boasts Britain's best vegan scene, a fact frequently translating to cheap eats. That's certainly true at *Chaiwalla*, a vegan Indian joint selling delectable chickpea curries and chana dals for around a fiver. Though visitors can't eat in, that caveat is entirely tolerable given Kingsmead Square's plane trees and Green Park's riverside are within a five-minute stroll. Consider also *JC's Kitchen*, a Filipino street food van currently based by Bog Island whose good portions of marinated pork belly with cheesy bubble and squeak cost £7.

42 Monmouth Street (+44 7926 041588, www.instagram.com/chaiwallabath); Terrace Walk (+44 7841 649857, www.jcskitchen.co.uk)

🔔 SPLASH OUT

Bath's fulsome fine dining scene has been further beefed out by a newish collaboration between culinary godfathers Pierre Koffmann and Marco Pierre White at The Abbey Hotel. More brasserie than formal restaurant, *Koffmann and Mr White's* serves English and

▲ A joint venture between two culinary greats, Koffmann and Mr White's serves a mix of English and French classics.

▼ Clayton's Kitchen prides itself on refined modern French cuisine presented to perfection.

French flavor fare, such as braised ox cheeks beside apple purée. Eat out in its garden if it's warm. Other options include Acorn, a posh vegetarian option proffering five course tasters, and under the radar *Clayton's Kitchen*, where bright, uncluttered interiors align with the unfussy, top-notch fare. Fillet steaks alongside duck fat chips are a guilty pleasure, as are passion fruit crème brûlées.

North Parade (+44 1225 461603, www.abbeyhotelbath.co.uk); 15a George Street (+44 1225 585100, www.claytonskitchen.com)

PUB PERFECTION

Beer hounds are best served by heading north to **Chapter One**, a bright community pub in Camden with a constantly changing list of craft beers on draft from local, independent breweries. You'll also find board games, from Carcassonne to Uno, but no screens showing sports. Hop fanatics determined to stay more central are directed to the Beercraft store, which stocks 550 global tipples. And those more inclined toward pub grub should make for family run **The Raven**, a Georgian townhouse beauty whose nine daily pie options are accompanied by a choice of gravies and creamy mash or chips—yum!

Lower East Hayes (www.chapteronebath.co.uk); 7 Queen Street (+44 12 2542 5045, www.theravenofbath.co.uk)

BRILL FOR BRUNCH

On the elegant Upper Borough Walls, just a minute or two from Bath Abbey and Pulteney Bridge in the city's brown stone heart, **Good Day Café** is a cool café putting the emphasis on local suppliers. Alongside quality coffee and wicked pastries, its all-day brunch menu spans bacon bagels and toasted banana bread under blueberry compote. Service is

warm and the upstairs room—pale pink walls, neon signs, and succulents—a visual dream. If you're feeling bold or need a pick-me-up, order a charcoal or beetroot latte with your meal. Dogs are welcome.

12 Upper Borough Walls (+44 1225 684284, www.gooddaycoffee.co.uk)

KILLER COCKTAILS

With ingredients "foraged from the lush and bountiful hills that surround this fine city," **The Dark Horse** sounds more like an on-trend restaurant. Instead it's a seductive, subterranean cocktail den whose mixology prioritizes West Country flavors. There's lots to like: the lighting is low, the staff friendly, the music jazz or soul, and the seasonal menu long, extending to Orange Groves (gin, clementine liqueur, apricot,

▲ A cozy cocktail den, The Dark Horse uses many English liquors to create their cocktails.

lemon, pale ale) and Ten Cent Pistols (bourbon, banana, bitters, lapsang-infused honey, and lemon). More mainstream but similarly good is **Circo** on George Street; it produces its own bitters and holds regular cocktail making classes.

7a Kingsmead Square (+44 1225 282477, www.darkhorsebar.co.uk); 15–18 George Street (+44 1225 585100, www.circobar.co.uk)

REGIONAL FAVES

The Sally Lunn bun isn't really a bun at all; it's brioche best served lightly toasted and slathered in cinnamon butter. That's how they do it at the rich delicacy's home, anyhow. Probably Bath's oldest building, **_Sally Lunn's Historic Eating House_** dates back to 1482 and has beamed dining rooms. A small museum also reveals what's known about the mysterious—and possibly fictional—Lunn. Similarly elusive, oddly, are Bath Chaps: pork tongues wrapped in pork cheeks, marinated, baked, and rolled in breadcrumbs. Track them down as a bar snack at the cozy **_Garrick's Head_** pub, beside Theatre Royal.

4 North Parade Passage (+44 1225 461634, www.sallylunns.co.uk); 7–8 St John's Place (+44 1225 318368, www.garricksheadpub.com)

☕ **CAFFEINE KICKS**
Various things proliferate in Bath: cameras, cobbles, Georgian buildings, hills, sighs of wonder, and, happily, quality coffee. Despite the impressive artisan claims of Society, Mokoko, Picnic, and the beautiful Cascara, the ultimate temple is **_Colonna & Small's_**, a stripped back store cofounded by three-time UK barista champion Maxwell Colonna-Dashwood. His changing seasonal menus here call on a variety of countries, using scientific equipment and roasteries across the land. Should coziness be a key consideration, consider **_The Colombian Company_** run by Jhampoll Gutierrez Gomez, which strictly uses speciality, sustainable, and fair trade green beans from the South American country.

6 Chapel Row (+44 7766 808067, www.colonnaandsmalls.co.uk)

6 Abbey Gate Street (+44 7534 391992, www.thecolombiancompany.com)

▲▶ Sally Lunn's is a world famous tea and eating house and one of the oldest houses in Bath, whose best known bake is the Sally Lunn bun, which is served with lashings of cinnamon butter.

🧳 SUITCASE SWAG

Held every Saturday from 9am to 1.30pm below the disused Green Park station building's arched glass ceiling, the *Bath Farmers' Market* ranks among the region's best. Attendees rotate, of course, so you'll just have to hope that Wainwright's organic forest honey, Moist's beetroot hummus, or The Orgasmic Jam Co's apple and cinnamon flavor are available. Or you could check the website. Back centrally, *The Fine Cheese Co* hawks lots of condiments and assortment boxes alongside bries, blues, and everything in between at a shop and café—helping it narrowly outstrip Paxton & Whitfield as the city's premier cheesemonger.

▲The Beckford Bottle Shop is a bistro offering sumptuous small plates, cheese, and charcuterie, as well as an abundance of wine.

Green Park Station (www.bathfarmersmarket.co.uk); 29–31 Walcot Street (+44 1225 448748, www.finecheeseshops.co.uk/bath)

🥂 DATE FOR TWO

Okay, so there's no view of the Eiffel Tower or Sacre Coeur, but Bath's best bistro still delivers pretty vistas of the city's Pulteney Weir, making it perfect for lovers. Small and family run, *Chez Dominique* dishes up wholesome European dishes cooked very well. Examples? Try the chicken breast with chorizo, cavolo nero, and a white bean, Basque-style piperade. No less intimate is the *Beckford Bottle Shop* that, despite its name, is a wine bar serving sharing plates to couples in quiet corners. Whether you opt for mackerel tartare on sesame crackers or wine-glazed ox cheek, the chocolate mousse is practically non negotiable.

15 Argyle Street (+44 1225 463482, www.chezdominique.co.uk); 5–8 Saville Row (+44 1225 809302, www.beckfordbottleshop.com/bath)

▼ Chez Dominique is a cozy and comfortable restaurant where simple ingredients are simply cooked to create delicious dishes.

TEA TIME

If your afternoon tea priority is atmosphere, there's only one place. Amid the Roman Baths complex, the *Pump Room Restaurant's* fluted columns, a giant crystal chandelier, and classical string trio almost put its nosh—from finger sandwiches to Battenberg sponge and chocolate éclairs—in the shade. Happily, that nosh is very good, including a Somerset High Tea with apple

▲ Treat yourself to a traditional afternoon tea at The Royal Crescent Hotel & Spa and enjoy a truly English experience.

jam, although still not quite as terrific as the crumbly scones and elaborate snacks unveiled at the sophisticated *Royal Crescent Hotel and Spa's Dower House Restaurant*. Offering sweet, savory, and vegetarian afternoon teas plus Taittinger fizz, this is the ultimate ladies-who-lunch haunt.

The Roman Baths, Abbey Church Yard (+44 1225 444477, www.romanbaths.co.uk; 16 Royal Crescent (+44 1225 823333, www.royalcrescent.co.uk/wine-dine)

Stow-on-the-Wold, Kingham,
and surrounding areas

ENGLAND

> Ignoring the major settlements—Cheltenham, Gloucester, and Cirencester—this guide concentrates on the rural Cotswolds, where chalk rivers and rolling hills conspire to produce a rich bounty of trout, lamb, Old Spot pork, wines, and more on which luxury hotels, chocolate box village tea rooms, former Blur guitar players, and a glut of gastropubs capitalize.

💲 ON A BUDGET?

Rather ironically, given that four-wheeled public transport is so elusive here, the Cotswolds' best cheap eats are found on a converted bus. Located in a lay by on the Cotswold Way footpath near Seven Springs, *The Cotswold Diner* does toasties, cooked breakfasts, and sandwiches for under £5, though nothing earns raver reviews than its cheeseburgers and sweet relish: the best in England according to one TripAdvisor critic. Equally revered is *Cotswold Baguettes*, in the typically pretty northern town of Stow-on-the-Wold. Don't be fooled by the name: as well as stuffed loaves at £4, this friendly café sells homemade scotch eggs, pasties, sausage rolls, and salad boxes.

Off A436, north of A435 roundabout (+44 7725 667304); Church Street (+44 1451 831362, www.cotswoldbaguettes.co.uk)

🔔 SPLASH OUT

Famously dubbed Britain's poshest pub, *The Wild Rabbit's* honey stone Cotswold walls frame chunky beams, open fireplaces, flagstone floors, and leather armchairs. Happily, this Kingham inn's food is also exceptional—as you might expect of somewhere owned by Daylesford honcho Lady Bamford. Her farm's organic food, seasonal game, and a Josper grill combine in wholesome, unfussy British dishes done splendidly. Down on the Cotswolds' southern fringes, executive chef Niall Keating earned two Michelin stars aged just 28 for his Asian- and French-inspired dishes at Whatley Manor's formal *Dining Room*. Stroll the gardens first, then settle down for the chef's menu in a lemon-hued restaurant.

Church Street, Kingham (+44 1608 658389, www.thewildrabbit.co.uk); Easton Grey (+44 1666 822888, www.whatleymanor.com)

▶ The Wild Rabbit is a great place to eat, drink, sleep, and be merry.

PUB PERFECTION

The Wild Rabbit is just one establishment that cements the Cotswolds as gastropub heaven; others include Burford's Lamb Inn, rural Northleach's Wheatsheaf Inn, and The Ebrington Arms. Two others particularly stand out, however. Near Nailsworth, south of Stroud, the cozy *Weighbridge Inn* serves "2-in-1" pies: half and half affairs with pastry wrapped fillings such as beef neighboring, say, cauliflower cheese. And out east in Ascott-under-Wychwood, new owners have seen *The Swan* cement its artsy prints and cool wallpaper with a more reliable food offering: homemade pies again, plus rib eyes and sea bream. The bar, low-ceilinged and fire-heated, is wonderfully comfortable.

Avening Road, Longfords (+44 1453 832520, www.weighbridgeinn.co.uk); 4 Shipton Road (+44 1993 832332, www.countrycreatures.com/the-swan)

BRILL FOR BRUNCH

Lady Bamford's HQ excels at brunch. Also notable for its shop and cookery school, *Daylesford's* brekkie offering mines the farm's bounty for your pleasure: maple and pecan overnight oats, scrambled eggs and kimchi on beetroot sourdough, or buttermilk pancakes alongside coconut yogurt. The quality of the ingredients is evident in every bite. Daylesford is up in the north-eastern Oxfordshire Cotswolds; in the south westerly reaches is Tetbury, a town best known for its antique shops. Providing succor to its heirloom hawkers is *Café 53*, whose Conquistador breakfast can be enjoyed on mismatched old furniture or in the garden.

Off A436, north of Kingham (+44 1608 731700, www.daylesford.com); 53 Long Street (+44 1666 502020, www.cafe53.co.uk)

▼ Rustic food is served in The Swan. Make sure to grab a spot by the fire for added coziness.

TIME FOR TEA

Amid so many classic Cotswolds villages and towns, Bourton-on-the-Water is perhaps the fairest of them all. As such, it clearly requires an indulgent tearoom, which is where **Smiths Kitchen** comes in. Occupying a listed stone building near the riverfront, it serves Traditional Cream Teas and stacked trays Afternoon Teas—the capital letters implying, rightly, that this is a serious matter— starring soft bakes, rich cakes, and far too much clotted cream. Even closer to water is the **Old Mill**, a museum and outdoor tearoom in Lower Slaughter where history, homemade scones, and soft jazz music come together beside the River Eye.

▲ An award-winning and family-run vineyard, Woodchester Valley is open all year long for tours and tastings.

Victoria Street (+44 1451 821401); Mill Lane (+44 1451 822245, www.oldmill-lowerslaughter.com)

PERPETUAL WINE

Deep in the Five Valleys, on the Cotswolds' southwestern fringes close to Stroud, family run **Woodchester Valley** began life in 2007 by trialing vines on one acre. Harvesting grapes from pinot noir to sauvignon blanc—with a wine using the latter regularly hoovering up awards—its three sites include a high-class production facility and offer two tours: a classic option and another themed to sparkling wine. Available all year, both must be pre-booked. Prefer a wider selection of tipples? Then head to **Lords of the Manor**, a posh seventeenth-century country hotel in Upper Slaughter and choose from their thousand-strong cellar.

Convent Lane (+44 7710 605558, www.woodchestervalleyvineyard.co.uk); Off Rose Row (+44 1451 604446, www.lordsofthemanor.com)

☕ CAFFEINE KICKS

Stow-on-the-Wold's toffee-hued edifices hide lots of history and, unexpectedly, something very modern and cool: the UK's smallest commercial coffee roastery (or so they reckon). Happily, for visitors, *Stow Town Coffee*—which uses green beans from estates around the planet—opens as an espresso bar with a cushy upstairs lounge, although hours are limited (8am–12pm on weekdays, and occasionally on Saturdays). Should the café be more important than the coffee, venture a few steps east to *Jaffé & Neale*, where Aga-baked carrot and banana cakes and a good bookshop append the cappuccinos. There's also an original branch in Chipping Norton.

▲ The Big Feastival food and music festival is organized by chef Jamie Oliver and Blur bassist Alex James on James' farm.

2 Wells Barn, Sheep Street (+44 1451 832519, www. stowtowncoffee.co.uk); 8 Park Street (+44 1451 832000, www. jaffeandneale.co.uk)

🎪 BEST FEST

Every August, Blur bassist come celebrity cheesemonger Alex James hosts *The Big Feastival* on his farm near Kingham. His pulling power ensures a star-studded epicurean line up; in 2019, for instance, Mark Hix, *British Bake Off* champ Candice Brown, and Raymond Blanc all rocked up. Just as good is the music, with last year's headliners Rudimental, Jess Glynne, and Elbow all performing. Pop-up restaurants and a food market selling, among other things, James'

◀ Jaffé & Neal combines a bookshop with quality coffee and cake.

Blue Monday cheese, complete the fun. And if you're averse to all things untidy, fear not—this festival's vibe is more truffled haloumi fries than piss-puddled Portaloo.

www.thebigfeastival.com

🥂 DATE FOR TWO

Whatever you do, go Wild. Not at The Wild Rabbit, although that's entirely romantic, but at *Wild Thyme*, a Chipping Norton restaurant whose superior Mediterranean British fusion—double-baked gorgonzola soufflé, mac and cheese alongside a duck entrecote, and savoy cabbage—is available to just 35 diners in candlelit, stone-walled surrounds. Or at Nailsworth's *Wild Garlic*, where bright wallpaper and patterned cushions create an amorous feel, especially if you ask for a corner table. The bistro menu extends to boards to share, summer salads, and house made pastas—such as the pappardelle with an overnight braised venison and date ragout. Yum.

▶ The Wild Thyme is run by a husband-and-wife team and serves modern, British food with Mediterranean influences.

10 New Street (+44 1608 645060, www.wildthymerestaurant.co.uk); Chestnut Hill (+44 1453 832615, www.wild-garlic.co.uk)

🧳 SUITCASE SWAG

A converted barn in rolling arable fields outside Moreton-in-Marsh, the family owned *Cotswold Food Store and Café* has wooden crates full of produce from nearby farms. There are cheeses and pork pies, too, while the onsite restaurant tempts with light lunches. Not far north, in yet another picture-perfect village, the

Broadway Deli's shelves bulge with the same sort of stuff, plus an excellent range of jams, chutneys, and condiments. Food is also served. If you're consigned to the southern Cotswolds, Saturday morning's Stroud Farmers' Market—sometimes attended by a certain Damien Hirst—has all your kitchen or gift needs covered.

A424 near Longborough (+44 1451 830469, www.cotswoldfoodstore.com); 29 High Street (+44 1386 853040, www.broadwaydeli.co.uk)

71

Ludlow

ENGLAND

> Famously lauded as "the loveliest town in England" by poet John Betjeman, Ludlow assembles its half-timbered houses in a crook of the River Teme. You've also got the ruined castle and dark green Shropshire Hills all around. Yet for all that, food has long been visitors' chief reason to come here, with everything from mysterious pies to sausage trails on offer.

💲 ON A BUDGET?

Handily near the castle, *Aragons* is a café that usually punches above its weight. Not everything is perfect but, chances are—whether it's their homemade faggots, pizza, paninis, pesto chicken with mash, quiches, calzone, or veggie burgers—that the cooking will be good. Prices are low by, er, Ludlow standards, with everything currently under a tenner, and service eternally warm. The same goes for the slightly pricier *Golden Moments*, a South Asian restaurant popular with chef Shaun Hill (see *Abergavenny*, pages 134–139) when he ran the Michelin-starred Merchant House. Expertly done chicken, lamb, and prawn curries cost £10–15 with rice.

5 Church Street (+44 1584 873282); 50 Broad Street (+44 1584 878488, www.goldenmomentsofludlow.co.uk)

🔔 SPLASH OUT

During the nineties and noughties, Ludlow had three Michelin-starred restaurants (including Merchant House); now, with the relevant places closed or chefs moved on, it has zero. No matter though because there's still some esteemed fine dining to dress up for. Chiefly at *Mortimers*, which mines fresh Shropshire ingredients in a menu fusing modern British tricks with vintage French philosophy. Across an eight-course tasting menu, which translates to such delights as sea trout with a crab bonbon or guinea fowl alongside Wye Valley asparagus. Low ceilings, oak panels, and exposed stone walls set an agreeably historical tone, with garden seating available when the weather is warm.

17 Corve Street (+44 1584 872325, www.mortimersludlow.co.uk)

PUB PERFECTION

Adhering faithfully to the English town manual, Ludlow is packed with pubs. There's the cobbled, china-filled Rose & Crown; there's the community-hub Church Inn just next door; there's the low-beamed, positively prehistoric Unicorn, its garden by the wispy River Corve, and there's parlor room The Dog Hangs Well, only open from Thursday through Sunday. Then there's **The Charlton Arms**, a foodie haunt next to arched Ludford Bridge where French owner Cedric Bosi oversees an uncomplicated menu that has earned Bib Gourmand recognition from those Michelin folk. Try to leave space for the potted rhubarb cheesecake.

Ludford Bridge (+44 1584 872813; www.thecharltonarms.co.uk)

DATE FOR TWO

Every half-competent lothario knows that Parisian bistros make the most romantic restaurants. Happily, for Ludlovian lovers, **The French Pantry** has pretty much replicated their recipe—pools of yellow light, soft chatter, quiet corners, careful cooking—and thrown in a fairylight patio to boot. Expect Gallic classics such as *moules marinière* and *tarte tatin*, supported by a small army of wines. Just as intimate is popular **Chang Thai,** whose colorful décor enlivens an old

▲ Blossoming bistro, The French Pantry, offers Ludlow locals a small menu that changes daily.

► A family- and friends-run business, Chang Thai serves tasty and traditional Thai dishes.

pub. Across two rooms of varying formality it serves Thai tapas, authentic mains like fried duck with tamarind sauce, a shower of cashew nuts, and fun cocktails.

15 Tower Street (+44 1584 879133, www.thefrenchpantry.co.uk); 3 Market Street (+44 1584 874212, www.thailudlow.co.uk)

REGIONAL FAVES

Ever had fidget pie? Neither has most of Ludlow, apparently. That was the conclusion of a *Vice* article in 2017 entitled "Why Has No One in Shropshire Heard of Shropshire Fidget Pie?" One place that certainly has is the **Ludlow Farmshop**, a sort of deli-cum-supermarket which, despite its name, is in

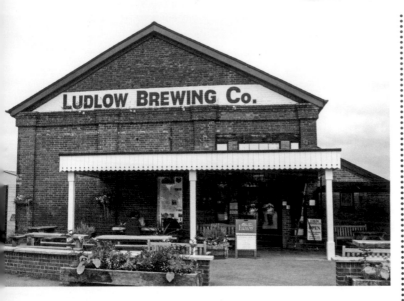

Ludlow Brewing Company is keen to maintain the town's long tradition of brewing.

BRILL FOR BRUNCH

Under the patronage of Clive Davis, The Green Cafe earned a name for fresh, dynamic and drop-dead-cheap café cooking, most of it homemade and all of it brilliant. Now under new owners, *CSONS at The Green Cafe* is a bit pricier and has put more emphasis on the all-round product. That's particularly evident on morning visits, when the breakfast menu offers granola with lemon curd or spicy Mexican eggs. The coffee, from a Shropshire Hills roaster, is Ludlow's best, and the restored watermill setting idyllic. For something simpler, visit *Vaughans Sandwich Bar* and have a bacon or sausage sandwich of supreme quality.

Mill on the Green, Linney (+44 1584 879872, www.thegreencafe. co.uk); 14 King Street (+44 1584 875453, www.facebook.com/ ludlow14kingstreet)

the nearby village of Bromfield next to revived restaurant with rooms, The Clive Arms. Here, alongside venison and marmalades, awaits the muffin-sized dish. While its provenance is unknown, the ingredients are non-negotiable: gammon, apples, and cider (yes!) cooked in pastry, often with onion and potatoes, and, recently, a toupee of mash.

Bromfield, just off A49/Bromfield Road (+44 1584 856000, www.ludlowfarmshop.co.uk)

BEER OH BEER

Concocted inside a restored Victorian railway shed, the *Ludlow Brewing Company's* six options include an amber, a stout, and a citrus-note blonde. Daytime visitors are welcome, with a bar selling bottles from a bargain £1.60, while pre-booked tours, featuring samples of all beers and a free print, cost £7 and are available weekdays or Saturday afternoons. Beer-lovers might also order a bottle of treacly Shropshire Lad—from Wood's Brewery, ten miles north—in Aragons (see *On A Budget?*). It commemorates the centenary of AE Housman's sad, same-named poem cycle; Housman is buried here at St Laurence's Church.

The Railway Shed, Station Drive (+44 1584 873291, www. theludlowbrewingcompany.co.uk)

SUITCASE SWAG

Bring a big, big bag. You'll need it, not only for the Ludlow Farmshop, but for coffees, *pasteis de nata* tarts, or homemade rabbit rillette from the *Harp Lane Deli*; for pesto and walnut loaves from artisan bakery Swifts, and for blocks of nutty, hard Little Hereford from the Mousetrap Cheese Shop. And if you have time to drive 25 minutes (or take the train for 15) to quaint Church Stretton and *Van Doesburg*—one of England's greatest delicatessens—well then, bring an entire spare suitcase. The cakes and bakes here are especially godly.

4 Church Street (+44 1584 877353, www.harplane.com); 3 High Street, Church Stretton (+44 1694 722867, www.vandoesburgs.co.uk)

🍰 TEA TIME

Visiting Ludlow Castle? Though the Norman fortress was left to ruin in the seventeenth century, its ground floor has been restored for visitors, and its history is fascinating. The complex effectively served as the Welsh capital during the Marches era and was visited by Henry VIII's brother, Prince Arthur, during his honeymoon with Catherine of Aragon. Present-day visitors can also self-cater in an adjacent mansion or visit *The Castle Kitchen*. Despite no longer being called the "Tea Room," this glorified café still serves loose-leaf Earl Greys, fruit scones, lemon cakes, and the like.

Castle Square (+44 1584 878796, www.ludlowcastle.com/castle-shops)

🎏 BEST FEST

The *Ludlow Food Festival* began in 1995 when such events were rare—with its snaffling of such a desirable URL confirming as much. Some 20,000 visitors now descend on the ruined castle every September. They encounter 180 regional producers hawking whiskey, cheese, mango and gooseberry relish, and more, plus workshops, tastings, and household-name chefs and food writers giving demos or readings. Especially fun are beer and sausage trails, on which you can try nominated bangers or beers before voting for a favorite. Consider, too, two sister events: May's beer, music, and motor-themed Spring Festival and the Ludlow Magnalonga—a gastronomic hike— in August.

www.foodfestival.co.uk

▼ The original fair for food and drink lovers, Ludlow Food Festival continues to promote the area's producers year on year.

Birmingham

ENGLAND

> Curries, right? That's the popular perception of Britain's second city, borne on the famous Balti Triangle and a reputation for offering little more. But it's well out of date. For while Brum's curry scene remains buoyant, you'll also find one of the country's best craft-beer hubs and farmers' markets, plus seriously cool cocktail bars and wacky modern restaurants.

ON A BUDGET?

As a drab outdoor mall of Bonmarche and Boots outlets—plus lots of empty units—it's fair to say the Martineau Place makes for an unlikely foodie pilgrimage. But here, nonetheless, is Italian restaurant *La Vera*, whose pizzas are a fluffy revelation. Cooked in a wood-fired oven with crispy dough and good ingredients, their margheritas offer particularly tremendous value at £5.90. The same goes for Cantonese-style double-roasted duck curries or chicken with black bean sauce at Chinatown's *Look in Takeaway*. Meat, which gets roasted fresh every day, is unusually abundant and the rice made just right.

S16 Martineau Place (+44 121 233 1988, www.pizzerialavera.co.uk); 6 Ladywell Walk (+44 121 666 7587, www.facebook.com/lookinrestaurant)

CAFFEINE KICKS

Quarter Horse Coffee is worth the walk. Trot to Gay Village and Southside, about 15 minutes from New Street, and you'll happen on one of Britain's best roasteries.

▶ Medicine Bakery & Kitchen bakes a unique mix of hand-crafted artisan breads, cakes, and pastries.

Treating beans in plain sight using high-tech equipment, they produce long blacks, lattes and the like in cool surrounds. For something more exotic, Java Lounge, which uses Yemeni coffee—said by many to be the world's finest—has stores on Colmore Row and in Moseley. Or go to *Medicine Bakery + Kitchen* for an artisan kruffin or cronut with your cappuccino.

88–90 Bristol Street (+44 121 448 9660, www.quarterhorsecoffee.com); 69a New Street (www.medicinebakery.co.uk)

SPLASH OUT

Glynn Purnell is Birmingham's highest-profile chef, and **Purnell's** his central base. Though prices are high and there's a Michelin star, this isn't a stuffy place of white tablecloths: instead you get "nose-to-tail" cooking, personable waiters, and bravura menus. Haddock and eggs come with cornflakes and curry oil; the roast venison with a butternut-squash confit. Wackier still is **The**

Wilderness, which plays The Darkness and Black Sabbath as it manipulates high-end British fare. Smoked eels top charred potato, all coated in wild garlic and whey sauce; NAFB (Not Another F***ing Balti) involves a delicate quail samosa.

---

55 Cornwall Street (+44 121 212 9799, www.purnellsrestaurant.com); 27 Warstone Lane (+44 121 233 9425, www.wearethewilderness.co.uk)

BRILL FOR BRUNCH

With Yorks closing branches and Peel & Stone now just a wholesale supplier, **Gas Street Social** has assumed the mantle of Brum's brunch king. A position in the Mailbox shopping and office development has its patio facing the canal, which is very nice on sunny days. Nicer still are the American-style pancakes with streaky bacon, the avocado and eggs on toast, and the five-person Social Breakfast extravaganza. Bottomless boozy brunches are

▼ Purnell's takes inspiration from France and the Far East.

anchored on bellinis or mimosas, and there's good coffee, too. With New Street inside a ten-minute trot, it works well for a first or last weekend-break stop.

166–168 Wharfside Street (+44 121 643 0362, www.gasstreetsocial.co.uk)

PUB PERFECTION
Great pubs proliferate in Birmingham, but few are as relaxing as *The Church Inn*. In the historic Jewellery

▲ Post Office Vaults stocks beers from Belgium, Germany, France, Norway, Holland, Austria, and the USA amongst others, as well as traditional ciders and perries (a fermented beverage made of pears).

Quarter just northwest of the center, it includes a sun-drenched rooftop and a back-room pizza parlor. Lots of good ales are on tap. Talking of which, *Post Office Vaults*— whose name is partly misleading, with no envelopes or franking machines in sight; this is a subterranean den, though—has more than 250 bottled beers from every corner of the globe, plus draught

options and ciders. Food isn't served but you're welcome to bring your own, with plates and cutlery provided.

22 Great Hampton Street (+44 121 448 3866, www.inn-credible.co.uk); 84 New Street (+44 121 643 7354, www.postofficevaults.co.uk)

REGIONAL FAVES

A classic Black Country delicacy, faggots are meatballs blending minced offcuts, offal—usually pig's heart or liver—and herbs. Try them at **The Vine Inn**, or The Bull & Bladder as locals call it. Slightly outside of town in Brierley Hill and overseen by the Batham's brewery, the homely pub serves huge plates of faggots with mushy peas, chips, and gravy. Then there's Birmingham's most famous culinary creation. Balti is traditionally a mild lamb- or goat-meat curry, cooked in a thin pan. Head to the so-called Balti Triangle and **Adil's**, whose owner Mohammed Arif claims to have invented the dish in 1977.

---

10 Delph Road (+44 1384 78293, www.bathams.co.uk/pubs); 148–150 Stoney Lane (+44 121 449 0335, www.adilbalti.co.uk)

BEER OH BEER

Raspberry saison? Coconut porter? Ice-cream pale? These are some of the zanier offerings from Hockley brewery **Burning Soul**. All the main bases are covered, too, and visitors have two options: a taproom and garden open from 4–8pm on Fridays and 1–8pm on Saturdays— with a chance to try pilot

▲ 40 St Paul's is an award-winning, small and stylish bar boasting 140 gins.

beers—or hour-long tours on Saturdays at 1pm for £8. Look out too for Cotteridge Wines, one of Britain's finest bottle shops for beer, and **The Wolf**, a hipster pub of rotating guest beers on taps that are adorned with woodland animals.

Unit 1 Mott Street (www.burningsoulbrewing.com); 2–10 Constitution Hill (+44 121 212 9555, www.thewolfbirmingham.co.uk)

🍸 KILLER COCKTAILS

Using, improbably, a former side-street army barracks dating back to 1881 (of course), *1881* exemplifies the rangy mixology scene now found here. Amid walls lined with street art by Foka Wolf, drinks such as the pirate-themed Blackbeard's Revenge—dark rum, banana skins, and Caribbean spices—can be enjoyed across four-course tasting menus. Seasonal variations are also served, and they even have branded ice. If gin-based potions are your bag, make for *40 St Paul's* on Birmingham's last-remaining Georgian square: it was declared 2019's World Gin Bar of the Year by *Gin Magazine* and stocks some 140 options.

Thorp Street (+44 7802 364282, www.1881birmingham.co.uk); 40 Cox Street (+44 7340 037639, www.40stpauls.co.uk)

🏪 MARKET RESEARCH

A British Street Food Awards champion, *Digbeth Dining Club's* emporium has gone from pop-up to permanent. Open from Thursday through Sunday beside railway arches in bohemian Digbeth (which stretches east from Moor Street), its vendors sell cuisine from around the world and a lively atmosphere always

ensues. Further south, *Moseley Farmers' Market* occurs on the last Saturday of each month and sees 60 plus stalls sell everything from pineapples to pulled pork rolls. Everything is guaranteed to be local; no wonder this has won "Best Farmers' Market in the UK" three times.

Lower Trinity Street (www. digbethdiningclub.com); Alcester Road & St Mary's Row (www. moseleyfarmersmarket.org.uk)

💬 LOCAL SECRET

Beyond Balti, Birmingham is renowned for curry houses in general and many actually serve authentically Indian nosh. One of the best is *Raja Monkey* in Hall Green, a suburb some way to the southeast (get a train from Moor Street). Its dosas and puris are excellent, but neither rival the thali—a six-dish feast including rich Rajasthani mutton curry. Should curry not be your thing, then how about sushi? Run by a Pole—this is Birmingham, where diverse tribes come together, after all—*Gaijin Sushi* is a ten-seat Southside counter bar serving sensational plates at bargain prices.

1355 Stratford Road (+44 121 777 9090, www.rajamonkey.co.uk, closed Mondays); 78 Bristol Street (+44 121 448 4250, www. gaijinsushi.co.uk)

▲ *Digbeth Dining Club offers an authentic, unique experience where the street food does all of the talking.*

WELCOME TO
ALBERT DOCK

Liverpool

ENGLAND

> Ever since it was European Capital of Culture in 2008, Liverpool has been buoyant in its arts scene, its resurgent football team, and most definitely its food. And, cliché though it surely is, the one constant between its whole jerk chickens, seventies-style cocktail dens, beautiful boozers, and popcorn-dispensing coffee bars is a warmth of service rarely encountered elsewhere in Britain.

ON A BUDGET?

An excellent veggie/vegan joint, the hippie *Egg Cafe* (and gallery) occupies two levels of a purple painted Victorian warehouse in the creative Ropewalks district. Distinctly liberal and left

leaning in vibe, it throws in regular pie or pizza nights around standard menus encompassing leek and mushroom crumbles or beetroot and cashew curries, all of them under a tenner. Including a Michelin-starred

restaurant in this cost-cutting section might seem strange, yet Japanese establishment *Etsu*, near the Liver Building, unexpectedly dispenses lunchtime bento boxes for under £10—and whether you have sea bass, tuna, or chicken, each one generously comes with rice, salad, sauce, and potatoes.

16–18 Newington (+44 151 707 2755, www.facebook.com/ officialeggcafe); 25 The Strand (+44 151 236 7530, www.etsu-restaurant.co.uk)

SPLASH OUT

As pretty as the surrounding Georgian Quarter, *The Art School Restaurant's* twice-baked cheese soufflés, scallops with cauliflower purée, or roasted grouse breasts in thyme scented honey proudly showcase the best British ingredients. Its skylighted building was once a home for penniless children; today's tasting menus—with pescatarian and vegan versions—are very much for prosperous adults. Cooler and altogether more theatrical is nearby *Röski*, where *MasterChef: The Professionals* champ Anton Piotrowski also prioritizes homegrown grub. As The XX or Metronomy plays, 30 diners scoff such wonders as slow-cooked brisket joined by parsley powder, barbecued carrot, and "drunken," (read: beer marinated) onions.

1 Sugnall Street (+44 151 230 8600, www.theartschoolrestaurant. co.uk); 16 Rodney Street (+44 151 708 8698, www.roskirestaurant.com)

BEER OH BEER

Lots of Liverpool breweries have appeared in recent times as the craft beer charge intensifies. Among the best for visitors is *Love Lane*, repurposing a rubber factory in the Baltic Triangle. Tours of the shadowy premises run on Sundays and, at all other times, a bar serves the brand's pale ale alongside guest tipples, gin from a neighboring distillery,

sharing plates, and gourmet burgers. Up the "Golf Coast"— so-named for its many links courses—past sandy beaches and Antony Gormley's "Another Place" instalation is Formby's *Red Star Brewery*, offering Saturday tours and a bar touting everything from weissbier to oatmeal stouts.

62–64 Bridgewater Street (+44 151 317 8215, www. lovelanebrewing.com); 54b Stephenson Way (+44 1704 461120, www.redstarbrewery.co.uk)

MARKET RESEARCH

Opened in 2019, the *Duke Street Food & Drink Market* repatriates an old

building near Liverpool One into an all-day food court. Along Cuban, Asian, Italian, and vegan eats, plus three bars and a terrace, the headline act is Pilgrim, an Iberian restaurant inspired by the *Camino de Santiago* pilgrimage and a winner of BBC2's *My Million Pound Menu*. South of that begins the Baltic Triangle, an industrial area of workshops and garages gone cool, and not far inside is the whitewashed *Baltic Market*, whose street food treats extend to Neapolitan pizza, haloumi fries, and bubble waffles within a former brewery.

46 Duke Street (www.dukestreetmarket.com); Cains Brewery, Stanhope Street (www.balticmarket.co.uk)

▲The Art School Restaurant boasts a naturally lit dining room, champagne cellar bar, and stunning private wine tasting space.

▶ Liverpool's first street food market does not discriminate—all palates are welcome at Baltic, from fussy eaters to veggies, vegans, and meat lovers.

PUB PERFECTION

Various things make **The Shipping Forecast** great. There's its sworn promise of "non-hipster service;" there are its DJ sets, with Mark Ronson and Hot Chip among previous deck spinners; there's its Ropewalks location; its salvaged wood tables, and there's its huge menu, starring cheesy chili burgers and whole jerk chicken. The beer selection impresses too, with local indies beside Belgian head benders. Honorable mentions in this category go to **The Pheasant**, an award-winning gastropub up coast in Hightown, and **The Philharmonic Dining Rooms** —aka "The Phil"—for art-nouveau gates, wood panels, and stained-glass windows. You will never find a more beautiful boozer.

15 Slater Street (+44 151 709 6901, www.theshippingforecast liverpool.com); 20 Moss Lane (+44 151 929 2106, www. thepheasanthightown.co.uk); 36 Hope Street (+44 151 707 2837, www.nicholsonspubs.co.uk)

▶ The Shipping Forecast effortlessly combines food, drink, and live music (often from credible artists) to create a venue customers keep coming back to.

KILLER COCKTAILS

Jenny's began life as a speakeasy inside an eponymous fish restaurant. The latter has now been retired, and the groovy, '70s-inspired cocktail den given full focus. Expect colorful curtains, jungle wallpaper—the same one Elvis had in his New York hotel—intimate velvet booths, and turtlenecks galore, plus quirky libations. Pisco Inferno, blending pisco, elderflower cordial, fresh grapes, and pineapple, is a fruity fave. Newer, and more brooding in vibe, is **Present Company**, where savvy cocktaphiles order a Duster—dark rum, sherry, brown butter, and pecan caramel, yum. Cheesy crumpets can be called for should stomach-lining be in order.

The Old Ropery, Fenwick Street (+44 7535 684751, www. jennysliverpool.co.uk); 37–39 School Lane (+44 151 708 1827, www.presentcompany.bar)

CAFFEINE KICKS

Java zealots are directed to Bold St, to 92 Degrees, to Moose, and to Ropewalks' **Root Coffee**, which stands out by eschewing the millennial template of stark, small, and white in favor of snug, spacious, and wood-accented. Specialty guest brews—perhaps Copenhagen's April—rotate every few weeks. Still less textbook is the Ethiopian run **Coffee & Fandisha**, back in the Baltic Triangle. All its arabica is sourced from the African country, as is the tradition of partnering it with complimentary baskets of spiced popcorn (fandisha). Malt bread sandwiches and cakes are available too, while the "yellow wall" displays promote local artists.

52 Hanover Street (www. rootcoffee.co.uk); 5 Brick Street (+44 151 708 6492, www.coffeeandfandisha.com)

REGIONAL FAVES

Liverpudlians are known as Scousers because of "Lobscouse"—a stew, now also known as "scouse," reckoned to have been introduced by Northern European sailors and which contains root vegetables, beef, mutton, or chicken, and sometimes a pastry crust. Try it with meat or "blind" (a veggie version) alongside crusty bread at the *Baltic Fleet*, an ancient, CAMRA-backed pub beside the docks. Or indeed at *Fodder Canteen*, in the Baltic Triangle, where two other local dishes also await. Wet Nelly is a baked suet loaf traditionally made from bread scraps and dried fruit, and Liverpool Judy a lemon tart.

33a Wapping (+44 151 709 3116, www.facebook.com/thebalticfleetpub); 65 Norfolk Street (+44 151 352 3008, www.fodderliverpool.co.uk)

BRILL FOR BRUNCH

In (southerly district) Penny Lane, along with the Beatles' barbers and bankers, there is *The Tavern Co*—an instrument-crammed den whose full English has twice won national Best Breakfast awards. Available until 2.30pm are omelettes, sausage patties, and Nutella pancakes plus, fudging brilliant, free tea and

▲ Moose takes inspiration from the diners and delis of New York City with its American pancake stacks and Bronx Brunch.

coffee refills. Aforementioned under Caffeine Kicks, *Moose* also aces brunch: longer than some bibles, its American-style menu encompasses pesto eggs on toasted bagels and pulled pork hot dogs. The original Dale Street outpost is nicest. Also consider Leaf's three branches or The Baltic Bakehouse.

819–825 Smithdown Road (+44 151 734 5555, www.tavernco.co.uk); 6 Dale Street (+44 151 227 4880, www.moosecoffee.co)

DATE FOR TWO

The obvious shout here is posh Panoramic 34 for its sensational skyscraper views. But let's go obscure rather than obvious; let's talk instead about *Alma de Cuba*, a Victorian church

turned candlelit resto. Not only is there spunky South American and Caribbean to gobble—spicy salmon fishcakes and mojito lamb rumps—but red bricks and red carpets set an amorous tone. Alternatively, sweethearts inclined toward sharing plates and a buzzy-bistro feel should make for the exposed-brick square that is *Oktopus*, where fare like wild turbot with chive noisette, braised beetroot, and chocolate mousse cake have been acclaimed by Queen Marina O'Loughlin herself.

St Peters' Church, Seel Street (+44 151 305 3744, www.alma-de-cuba.com); 24 Hardman Street (+44 151 709 8799, www.oktopus-restaurant.com)

Manchester

ENGLAND

> Time was when all the great restaurants were in London. That time has passed and so has the subsequent one where cities like Manchester played catch up. Now restaurateurs are moving here, and Manchester pizzerias are branching out cross-country, their name made. Quality has seen off quantity, and "atmosphere," "innovation," and "fun" are the buzzwords.

ON A BUDGET?
With new branches in Birmingham and Liverpool, Manchester pizzeria *Rudy's* is now embarking on world domination. Quite right, too, given its Neapolitan principles of 24-hour-proved doughs, clay ovens enabling blistering blast cooks, sweet San Marzano tomato sauces, interesting toppings such as Tuscan

sausage and *friarielli* (bitter broccoli), and its prices— margheritas, for instance, are a piffling £6.50. The original outpost, in up-and-coming district Ancoats, is most fun; get there early to dodge a queue (it's walk-ins only) and consider a local craft beer or spritz cocktail to wash down your meal.

9 Cotton Street (+44 161 820 8292, www.rudyspizza.co.uk/ ancoats)

▼ Rudy's is all about the pizza—their dough is made on site every day, takes 24 hours to prove, 60 seconds to cook, and approximately 5 seconds to eat!

SPLASH OUT

After replacing Simon Rogan at the Midland Hotel's restaurant, 2016's *Great British Menu* winner has taken things in a more playful direction. Amid gray-green tones and cylindrical chandeliers, **Adam Reid at The French's** signature six-course *dégustations* might include bread-crumbed pig's trotters in rich umami with pickled-onion purée or a white chocolate mousse. They cost from £90. Still more casual in vibe is the UK fare-championing and Michelin-starred restaurant **Mana**. Its rare ingredients— desiccated spruce and reindeer moss—and minimal feel are explained by Simon Martin's

résumé: he spent two years cooking at Noma. Seasonal tasting menus, cooked in an open kitchen, are £105.

16 Peter Street (+44 161 235 4780, www.the-french.co.uk); 42 Blossom Street (+44 161 392 7294 www.manarestaurant.co.uk)

PUB PERFECTION

If you like it old-school, you'll love **The Smithfield Market Tavern** just off the hipster Northern Quarter. A homely place of dartboards, bands, and pork pies, it primarily serves Blackjack Brewery blends: 12 keg beers, six rotating cask ales, and bottles galore. Not to mention

ciders—this is, in fact, CAMRA's reigning Cider Pub of the Year. Similar charms await in the **Marble Arch Inn** up in historic Angel Meadow, along with classy cook looks courtesy of tiled walls and floors. Cheeseboards, pints of award-winning Lagonda IPA (from the pub's Marble Brewery), and a sunny garden all help days to pass pleasantly.

37 Swan Street (+44 161 425 6831, www.the-smithfield-market-tavern.business.site); 73 Rochdale Road (+44 161 832 5914, www.marblebeers.com)

BRILL FOR BRUNCH

Homemade, treacly banana bread, spiced with cinnamon and nutmeg, then topped in vanilla mascarpone; cheddar corn fritters and a pile of bacon; French toast under a berry compote, plus some white chocolate and almond crumble. All reasons to skip breakfast and make a mid-morning visit to the Northern Quarter and its antipodean-run original **Federal Cafe Bar**. Ozone coffee and a comfy room of pot plants and mustard-colored banquettes help, too. If Federal is full, skedaddle a few streets east to **Teacup**, co-owned by legendary DJ, Mr Scruff, and serving rarebits involving sourdough toast and Applewood cheese.

9 Nicholas Croft (+44 161 425 0974, www.federalcafe.co.uk); 53–55 Thomas Street (+44 161 832 3233, www.facebook.com/teacupnq)

▼ Teacup began its life as a record shop and has since transformed into a foodie favorite in Manchester's Northern Quarter.

REGIONAL FAVES

The region's best-known meal is forever associated with Manchester's most famous TV show. On *Coronation Street*, Betty opened the Rovers Return Inn and served Lancashire hotpots. In 2012, one of the soap's stars, Jennie McAlpine, launched a real life, city center restaurant, ***Annies***, and the same dish—a stew of lamb or mutton and onion, topped with sliced potatoes and slow-baked in a heavy casserole pot—remains a bestseller. Manchester is also known for Eccles cake and Manchester tart, a coconut, custard, and jam concoction, and both can be bought at ***Robinsons*** bakery if you take a trip northwest to Failsworth.

---

5 Old Bank Street (+44 161 839 4423, www.anniesmanchester. co.uk); 69/71 Ashton Rd East (+44 161 681 2493, www.robinsonsbakery.co.uk)

BELL ON BEER

For the best barometer of Manchester's craft beer scene (or, to paraphrase the rhyming slogan, if you fancy a drink), head to ***The Brink***. Every cask or keg beer and cider served at this basement micropub is made within 25 miles by artisan producers and staff know their stuff. It's also a refreshingly simple place of

▲ Bundobust offers a modern update to the classic "beer and curry" with authentic Indian dishes and boundary-pushing beers to whet the appetite.

wood tables and photo-crammed walls. Rather more unusual is ***Bundobust***, a vegetarian and also subterranean Gujarati restaurant, which does a fine

sideline in hoppy treats. Collaborations with local breweries and those from Leeds—from where Bundobust hails—inform its 16 taps.

---

65 Bridge Street (+44 161 834 6346, www.brinkmcr.co.uk); 61 Piccadilly (+44 161 359 6757, www.bundobust.com/manchester/)

🍸 KILLER COCKTAILS

Above the shopping and financial district Spinningfields stands *20 Stories*, a fine-dining restaurant with football player prices and cocktail bar, whose plant-filled terrace overlooks all of Manchester and is magic at night. The name is a pun, relating to the dishes' provenance, except it isn't, since this is the, er, nineteenth storey. Perhaps it'll make sense after a Major Birds Brandy Punch (cognac, lemon sherbet, and nutmeg)? Or perhaps you should go to cool, busy Spanish tapas restaurant *El Gato Negro* and get stuck into a margarita or Parma Violet (crème de violette liqueur, limoncello, cherry bitters, and cava) instead.

▲ Situated on the nineteenth floor, 20 Stories' glamorous restaurant, lively bar, and expansive rooftop terrace offer unrivaled 360-degree views of the Manchester skyline.

1 Hardman Square (+44 161 204 3333, www.20stories.co.uk); 52 King Street (+44 161 694 8585, www.elgatonegrotapas.com/manchester)

☕ CAFFEINE KICKS

This being the 2020s and Manchester being a major city, quality coffee abounds. Picking a standout is tough, but the railway arch-situated *ManCoCo* (Manchester Coffee Company) deserves acclaim for also being a microroaster that offers a wide range of seasonal, ethically sourced blends in southerly party district, Deansgate Locks. Takk, inside Hatch (see *Market Research*), and the food-serving Idle Hands are also good shouts. If delicacies are important then go to the Northern Quarter's Siop Shop for wondrous donuts or the Scandi-style *Pollen Bakery*, beside New Islington Marina, to scoff lemon and poppy seed cake or salted caramel brownies—delicious.

84 Hewitt St (+44 161 237 1916, www.mancoco.co.uk); Cotton Field Wharf, 8 New Union St (www.pollenbakery.com)

LOCAL SECRET

Yuzu deceives people by looking utterly utilitarian. Yet this Japanese joint's Loch Duart salmon sashimi bowls have won awards, its crispy fried kara-age chicken with ponzu sauce is just as raved-about, and its rice is as good as rice gets. Beautiful sashimi and noodle bowls are also offered and bebop plays. Why? Because. Talking of incongruities, Manchester's chunky Chinatown formerly housed—inside a supermarket—a Thai café called Siam Smiles. Rising rents forced a sad closure, but it has now reopened as *Thai Smiles* at the Great Northern Warehouse, serving the same beloved pork bellies and papaya salads with baby salted crabs.

39 Faulkner Street (+44 161 236 4159, www.yuzumanchester.co.uk); Deansgate Mews (+44 7702 741759, www.facebook.com/thaismilescafe)

MARKET RESEARCH

Near Manchester and Manchester Metropolitan universities on Oxford Road, *Hatch* is a market of multicolored shipping containers specializing, as many do, in street food. Vendors change every few months, but expect a hipster blend of cocktail haunts, "nano breweries," vegan bao buns, and fried chicken. A self-contained courtyard is heaven when the sun's out, and most outlets stay open all week.

Repurposing a beautiful two-tier, glass-roofed iron hall from the nineteenth century Smithfield Market atop the Northern Quarter, *Mackie Mayor* has a similar line-up of permanent providers hawking everything from chargrilled fish to flat iron steaks.

Oxford Road (www.hatchmcr.com); 1 Eagle Street (www.mackiemayor.co.uk)

▼ Housed in this Grade II listed market building, Mackie Mayor is the perfect place to while the day away, providing a whole host of breakfast, brunch, lunch, and dinner options.

Malton, Harrogate,

and surrounding areas

ENGLAND

> Everyone goes to York but why stop there? Further north are handsome foodie hubs like Harrogate and Malton, plus legendary gastropubs, gourmet hotels, and the producers of Wallace and Gromit's favorite crumbly cheese. As if that wasn't good news enough, the spectacular presence of the Dales and the Moors means it's easy to walk off each day's overindulgence.

💰 ON A BUDGET?

Ten pounds might seem a lot for a sandwich—but not when it's this good, this big, and this filling. Named after and inspired by the local owner's Norwegian grandmother, large Harrogate café *Baltzersens* does open sandwiches served with potatoes and house salad; the best is the meatball version, enlivened by fried onions, lingonberry jam, and Jarlsberg cheese. Mackerel pâté on rye toast (£8) and soups (£7) are also available. Even more of a bargain awaits in the charming beach resort of Whitby, at its *Humble Pie 'n' Mash Shop* in flavors from steak and stout to roasted veg and goats' cheese.

22 Oxford Street (+44 1423 202363, www.baltzersens.co.uk); 163 Church Street (+44 1947 606444, www.humblepie.tccdev.com)

▲ A former coaching inn, The Yorke Arms is now a Michelin-starred restaurant.

🔔 SPLASH OUT

North Yorkshire's grandest eats await in two cool, luxury hotels. Glammest is Grantley Hall, a Palladian-style house outside Ripon. As well as Japanese gardens and a spa, it has various restaurants headlined by *Shaun Rankin at Grantley Hall*. Here, having returned home, the previously Michelin-starred chef offers a "Taste of Home" degustation featuring gourmet riffs on such childhood staples as bilberry sandwiches and beef tea. Also accentuating local fare is Frances Atkins at *The Yorke Arms*, a converted eleventh-century cheesery in the Upper Nidderdale Valley. Her menus alter daily, but might feature Whitby crab, truffled cauliflower, or fall's first grouse in a bramble sauce.

◀ The Humble Pie 'n' Mash Shop offers an affordable and diverse menu of free-range and organic pies.

Near Grantley, on B6265 (+44 1765 62 0070, www.grantleyhall.co.uk); Ramsgill-in-Nidderdale (+44 1423 755243, www.theyorkearms.co.uk)

In the late 2000s, Tom Naylor-Leyland—whose family owns much of the town—decided to reinvent handsome Malton as "Yorkshire's food capital." A decade later, oodles of independent producers, a popular annual Food Lovers' Festival, and endorsement from the late Antonio Carluccio shows he has been true to his word. Central to a thriving food scene is the *Malton Monthly Food Market*, held on the second Saturday from March through November. Approximately 35 specialist food stalls and street food vendors hold forth on Market Place, hawking broad bean fritters, hedgerow gin, posh sausage rolls, and more.

www.visitmalton.com/food-market-yorkshire

▲ The Star Inn at Harome is a Michelin-starred gastropub serving modern Yorkshire food.

▼ Held every second Saturday, Malton Food Market is made up of 35 specialist food stalls and street food vendors.

PUB PERFECTION

North of Malton, and just off the hiker friendly Howardian Hills, is *The Star Inn at Harome*, a fourteenth-century thatched village hostelry heralded by Michelin. Chef-patron Andrew Pern was an early adopter of local sourcing—before every hipster and his post-ironic dog hopped aboard—and that translates here, in particular, to moorlands game and pasture-fed meat; hence the partridge and creamed sprouts, or the honey roasted duck with tea seasoned quail's eggs. A full vegetarian menu is provided, as are lots of port and cheese, and it's all wonderfully comfy and informal. Booking ahead is near vital.

High Street (+44 1439 770397, www.thestaratharome.co.uk)

and the pretty market town of Hawes. Specifically, at the **Wensleydale Creamery**, where a shop peddling over 20 varieties tempts alongside cheese making experiences and the chance to view ancient production equipment. Back toward Ripon, equally lovely Masham hoards the independent **Black Sheep Brewery**, whose extensive range stretches to chocolate and orange stouts and ruby ale Riggwelter, which, nudge nudge, go very well with Wensleydale. Tasting tours, a bar, and a shop await.

Gayle Lane (+44 1969 667664, www.wensleydale.co.uk); Gun Bank (+44 1765 680101, www.blacksheepbrewery.com)

🍽 BRILL FOR BRUNCH

Inspired by the hip East London area, and founded by relocated Londoners, **Hoxton North** is a buzzy place for Harrogate's hip young families and creative crowd. And anyone else, really, thanks to a very welcoming vibe; the only challenge is getting a table, with reservations not taken and crowds common. Available until 3pm, brunch menus span all the classic egg dishes, avocado options, sweet brioche French toast, posh fry ups, banana granola, and naughty Belgian chocolate suffused porridges. Specialty coffee and Origin hot chocolates headline the drinks card, with cocktails dispensed from midday onwards.

1 Royal Parade
(www.hoxtonnorth.com)

🍲 REGIONAL FAVES

Acclaimed by George Orwell, named in Monty Python, and immortalized in Wallace and Gromit, crumbly Wensleydale's spiritual home is an eponymous Yorkshire valley

▼Wensleydale Creamery's cheese shop stocks over 20 varieties of handcrafted cheese as well as everything to go with it.

DATE FOR TWO

If you drop into **Manchega** in Ripon, the welcome will be so warm that you'll wonder if you've been before. A family-run tapas restaurant, its extensive menu runs to haloumi salad with pine nuts and fig jam, pancetta wrapped dates, and cumin-marinated pork. Everything is decidedly moreish and fun, just as in the plant pot filled dining room of **The Talbot**, Malton's cooled-up coaching inn. Deviled kidneys on buttery sourdough are a favorite here, while sticky toffee *ginger* pudding offers a tart twist on the pudding classic.

1 Duck Hill (+44 1765 647554,

▲ Set in the award-winning foodie town of Malton, The Talbot cooks delicious fare, including Twice Baked Dale End Cheddar Soufflé.

www.manchega.co.uk); Yorkersgate (+44 1653 639096, www.talbotmalton.co.uk)

SUITCASE SWAG

Above all, though, Malton has brilliant food shops. The best might be **Malton Relish**, an artisan delicatessen stocking a broad range of locally sourced food: sausage rolls, chutneys, biscuits, and bakes. Head along The Shambles or down Market Place and you'll also happen on Yo Bakehouse's frangipane tarts, rabbit pies in Costello's Bakery, and the handmade

chocolates of Victorian confectioners Mennells. In Talbot Yard, where businesses use old stables, Florian Poirot (no relation) produces nationally acclaimed macaroons. Over by the Dales in Ripon, the 150-year-old **Appleton's Butchers** is known for selling the best pork pies for miles around.

58 Market Place (+44 1653 699389, www.maltonrelish.co.uk); 6 Market Square (+44 1765 603198, www.appletonsbutchers. co.uk)

TEA TIME

North Yorkshire's most famous foodie outpost? That'll be **Bettys**, a Harrogate tearoom dating back to 1919 and permanently held in high esteem for its sublime cakes. The first outpost was in Harrogate and—though now at a new, bigger premises—a café there remains the hub of a six-strong empire. It's open all day, but there's really only one time to visit: afternoons, when a cake trolley carries fruit tarts, lemon curd tortes, and more about the room. Those in the Dales should consider **Mill Race Teashop**, which not only has delicious fresh scones but sits beside the beautiful Aysgarth Falls.

1 Parliament Street (+44 1423 814070, www.bettys.co.uk); Yore Mill, Church Bank (+44 1969 663446, www.millraceteashop.com)

▲ Bettys is an institution and people travel from far and wide for a taste of its tea and cake.

CAFFEINE KICKS

The stylish red bricks of Talbot Yard are also home to speciality coffee roasters **Roost**, a husband-and-wife team who use a Diedrich machine to turn beans from Brazil, Rwanda, or elsewhere into their signature mix. Their premises also include a café in which one can sample the goods while perched on cushions fashioned from old sacks. Should sweet treats be called for, the Bluebird Bakery opposite makes brownies and millionaire's shortbread. Those based further west in the Dales should drive to Skipton, where **Bean Loved** promises well-trained baristas and mud from nearby hand roasters Dark Woods Coffee, who buy direct from small farmers.

6 Talbot Yard, off Yorkersgate (+44 1653 697635, www.roostcoffee.co.uk); 17 Otley Street (+44 1756 791534, www.beanloved.co.uk)

◀ Appleton's Butchers is best known for their pork pies, which have locals queuing round the market square.

Ambleside, Grasmere,

and surrounding areas

ENGLAND

> Ah, the lovely Lakes! Just as hearty fell walks and chugging boats are ten a penny here, so, too, are welcoming log-fire pubs and calorific tea rooms. But which are the best? And where to have dinner? What about if you're on a modest budget? Does anywhere do coffee? And where does that sticky toffee pudding come from? Here are all the answers...

ON A BUDGET?

Amid all the fells, flanks, woods, and water, it's easy to overlook the Lakes' towns. Kendal, for example, whose train station renders it a gateway, has pretty ancient lanes. It also has *Baba Ganoush*, a soup kitchen and imaginative vegetarian café serving spicy sausage stews and ciabattas with grilled mushroom, haloumi, avocado, and spinach. Mains are about £5. Beside a river near

Ambleside, chic **Chesters By the River** also has a strong veggie offering—try the sweet potato fritter with peanut salsa—plus pizzas, salads, and scones from an in-house bakery. Its cooking is excellent and prices uniformly low.

Unit 4 Berrys Yard, 27 Finkle Street (+44 1539 738210, www.instagram.com/ babaganoushkendal); Skelwith Bridge (+44 1539 434711, www.chestersbytheriver.co.uk)

SPLASH OUT

High-end eats abound, but there's no doubting the headliner. Occupying a former smithy in southerly Cartmel, two-Michelin-star **l'Enclume** is the flagship of Simon Rogan, an early pioneer of local sourcing. Rogan's epic tasting menu, priced at £155, raids his own 12-acre garden and involves earthy, theatrical flourishes—teeny mousses on compressed apple, say, or dollops of truffled yolk atop a Lakeland pebble. Up in Ambleside, James Cross' time at Noma has inspired a cool-climate approach at **Lake Road Kitchen** that strictly uses northern European ingredients. Expect Arctic cloudberries, 300-day-aged beef, and fried cauliflower alongside Finnish viili yogurt and pine.

Cavendish Street (+44 1539 536362, www.lenclume.co.uk); Lake Road (+44 1539 422012, www.lakeroadkitchen.co.uk)

PUB PERFECTION

Also abundant are pubs; expect wood beams, toasty fires, and low lighting as standard. For added history, try the **Poet's Bar** at The Lancrigg, a hotel near Grasmere (just outside, a memorial marks the spot where William Wordsworth uttered many of his poems and sister Dorothy transcribed them.) Walks to Easedale Tarn's

waterfalls can end here. In the lovely, lesser-visited Northern Lakes on Bassenthwaite's western side is **The Pheasant,** an historic inn crammed with locals, bitters, malts, and dogs. Its varnished walls' lustrous shade of crimson—caused by years of indoor smoking—has been declared impossible to recreate by designers.

Easedale Road (+44 1539 435317, www.lancrigg.co.uk/poets-bar); Bassenthwaite Lake, off A66 (+44 1768 776234, www.the-pheasant.co.uk)

▲ Expect nothing but the best seasonal and local ingredients from l'Enclume's fare. This two-Michelin-star restaurant uses the finest produce to create dishes such as this carrot and crab tart.

🍴 BRILL FOR BRUNCH

There's an irresistibly jolly quality to *The Old Sawmill Tearoom*, found between Bassenthwaite—which, trivia alert, is technically the only lake in the Lake District—and Keswick. That cheeriness comes from both its décor of polka-dot tablecloths and bunting and the fun nosh on offer—pork, bacon, and maple sausage rolls with homemade apple chutney, toasted Welsh Rarebit muffins alongside green-bean pickle, warm gingerbread plus rum butter, and so on, all available from 10am. Opt for a "shortbread squirrel," meanwhile, and you'll be helping local wildlife. Money for these goes toward the conservation of red squirrels in adjacent Dodd Wood.

Dodd Wood, off A591
(+44 1768 774317,
www.theoldsawmill.co.uk)

🍲 REGIONAL FAVES

The Lakes' most famous culinary confections have calories in common. First up is Grasmere gingerbread, a crunchier variation of the spicy-sweet cake devised by Victorian cook Sarah Nelson. Her original recipe is followed by descendants in the *Grasmere Gingerbread Shop*. To the east, energy-giving blocks of Kendal Mint Cake—a fixture of hikers' rucksacks—can be bought at the eponymous town's *Made in Cumbria* store. And Cartmel gives its name to a revered brand of sticky toffee pudding, sold in the same firm's *Cartmel Village Shop*. Talking of sticky toffee pudding, Ullswater's luxury *Sharrow Bay Hotel* restaurant says it invented the dish back in the 1970s—and still does a terrific version.

Church Cottage (+44 1539 435428,
www.grasmeregingerbread.co.uk);
www.madeincumbria.co.uk;
1 The Square (+44 1539 536280,
www.cartmelvillageshop.co.uk);
Howtown (+44 1768 486301,
www.sharrowbay.co.uk)

▼ The famous gingerbread from The Grasmere Gingerbread Shop is a spicy-sweet cross between a biscuit and a cake.

🍺 BEER OH BEER

They come to the rural *Kirkstile Inn*, northwest of Buttermere, for Tudor-era coziness born of ancient furniture and a carpeted, tongue-and-groove bar, and for food such as Cumbrian steak and ale pie. They come for rooms with four-poster beds. And they come for cask ales from an award-winning microbrewery (formerly onsite, now moved to cope with demand), including bitter and dark and golden concoctions—all perfect after a day's tramping or touring. If modern

▲ The Cheese Deli stocks a wide variety of cheese and, to go with them, cooked and cured meats, olives, chutneys, and crackers.

craft beers are your poison, try **Tweedies Bar** in Grasmere. Its Beer Bat offering sees a trio of guest beverages served in third-of-a-pint glasses.

Loweswater village (+44 1900 85219, www.kirkstile.com); Langdale Road (+44 1539 435300, www.tweediesgrasmere.com)

🧳 SUITCASE SWAG

In market town Keswick, **The Cheese Deli** stocks more than 90 different varieties—many of them Cumbrian—for sale. Among those representing the country are the nutty, buttery Blue Whinnow, crumbly white Coverdale (both from cow's milk), and the soft, mixed-milk Crofton. Cheese is also available just east of the Lakes—just off the M6—at

Tebay Services. Despite the taint of being a motorway pit-stop, this family-run institution doubles as an improbably terrific showcase for Cumbrian fodder across its café-restaurant, butchery, and, yes, southbound farmshop— where handmade cakes, pork pies, pre-packed sandwiches, and scotch eggs tempt.

9 Packhorse Court (+44 1768 773377, www.keswickcheesedeli. co.uk); M6 southbound between Junctions 38–39 (+44 1539 624511, www.tebayservices.com)

 DATE FOR TWO
The Drunken
Duck is romantic in a sublime, Hardyesque way, thanks to its position on a high, lonely crossroads outside Ambleside. On warm days, its beer garden offers fine fells views; otherwise, snuggle inside amid rugs and hanging hops. Despite the casual vibe, this is an award-winning gastropub serving serious, worldly cuisine. Take the lamb neck and spiced belly with freekeh, yogurt, and whey onions or filleted halibut accompanied by violet-artichoke confit. Similarly good—and secluded—is *The Cottage in The Woods*, a whitewashed restaurant with rooms on a tree-lined mountainside where

▲ As far as Lake District gastropubs go, the Drunken Duck Inn has it all—lush landscapes, locally inspired brews, and delicious restaurant dishes.

▼ The quality of The Cottage in the Woods' food and wine has won many awards and put them firmly on the culinary map.

you might eat rabbit with curried granola before a poached apricot rum baba.

Barngates (+44 1539 436347, www.drunkenduckinn.co.uk); Magic Hill, Whinlatter Forest (+44 1768 778409, www. thecottageinthewood.co.uk)

CAFFEINE KICKS

If the Lake District has a central hub it's Windermere, a town close to the large water of the same name. It's an excellent spot in which to stop and recharge; and the best place to do that is *Homeground Coffee + Kitchen*, where specialty, seasonal beans sourced from local roasters, Carvetii and Red Banks, are used. Skilled baristas prepare them, while

the trendy stone-and-wood interiors offer a cool alternative to the usual Lake District look book. Then there's the all-day brunch menu, spanning everything from huevos rancheros to apple and cinnamon donuts and buckwheat pancakes to bircher muesli.

Main Road (+44 1539 444863, www.homegroundcafe.co.uk)

TEA TIME

Lakeland's other forte is tearooms. If your priority is either the tea itself or the food alongside it, point your bonnet just south of the national park to Grange-over-Sands. There

you'll find *The Hazelmere*, whose rare leaf brews have scored Tea Guild awards and whose menu mines local fodder like Cumberland sausages and potted shrimps from adjacent Morecambe Bay. A bakery next door contributes Yorkshire curd tarts plus scones for afternoon teas. If you're less fussed about the food, try the *Tea Room* at The World of Beatrix Potter in Bowness-on-Windermere and scoff cake in the company of Peter Rabbit.

1–2 Yewbarrow Terrace (+44 1539 532972, www.thehazelmere.co. uk); Crag Brow (+44 1539 488444, www.hop-skip-jump.com)

▼ The Hazelmere takes great pride in their tea, matching it to your food, mood, and the time of day.

Dumfries and Galloway

SCOTLAND

> Dumfries and Galloway is easily missed. The A74 shoots right by, its oblivious drivers bound for Glasgow, the Lakes, or London as the region stretches away westward in bonny, forest-filled fashion. In its southerly reaches, beside Carlingwark Loch, you'll find its hub and "Scotland's designated food town"—designated by, er, the local council—Castle Douglas.

💰 ON A BUDGET?

Not content with winning "Best Fish N' Chips Establishment South West" at 2019's Food Awards Scotland gala, *Moore's Fish & Chips* went on to scoop the national category, too. On Castle Douglas' focal King Street—effectively the high street—it has been in the same family ever since Maureen and Walter Moore decided they'd tired of Glasgow, moved here, and opened in 1977. Their son Andrew runs the shop now, with that recent accolade one of a number pocketed. Haddock is a particular speciality. There's no seating, so perhaps take your packet to enjoy beside the loch.

254 King Street (+44 1556 502347, www. mooresfishandchips.co.uk)

🔔 SPLASH OUT

Inside a former Clydesbank Bank branch, diners now merrily pay upward of £50 for three courses at the newish *Mr Pook's Kitchen*. Pledging "Dumfries and Galloway on a plate," head chef Ed Pook is fond of foraged ingredients and, that buzz phrase again, "local produce." He also loves wizardry: evidence of this includes deep-fried duck eggs atop crispy squares of confit boar and lemon panna cottas with honeyed shortbread. Oh, and the venison chorizo, the pineapple gels, and the apple-tinged rum babas. A conversion has rendered the old bank airy and suitably modern; a contemporary temple to top-notch, fun-sponsored cooking. Playing it straighter is the acclaimed restaurant at *Trigony House*, a luxury country hotel and spa south of Dumfries. Everything—from gnocchi-style crab balls to honey and whiskey ice cream—is homemade, and again the accent is devoutly local.

---

38 King Street (+44 1556 504000, www.mrpooks.co.uk); Closeburn, off A76 (+44 1848 331211, www.trigonyhotel.co.uk)

LOCAL SECRET

In Dalry beside Galloway Forest stands *The Clachan Inn*, a snuggly haunt of the fire-heated, wood-paneled kind only found in rural Scotland. Amid its red-walled bar or dining room, you might eat salt and pepper squid with curry mayonnaise, or breaded Blackface lamb belly scrumpet alongside raw zucchini (courgette) or a duck breast and cherry reduction, and it will be ruddy wonderful, and it won't cost much at all. Such a scenario also applies to

The Pheasant, forty miles southwest in Sorbie. The equation here is simple: Neapolitan chef plus southern uplands produce equals unusual, award-winning riffs on Italian dishes from ravioli to pizza and pasta.

8–10 Main Street, St John's Town of Dalry (+44 1644 430241, www.theclachaninn.co.uk); 2 Wigtown Road (+44 1988 850270, www.thepheasantsorbie.com)

BEER OH BEER

From a King Street premises, *Sulwath Brewers* produce real ales and bitters following a traditional method with no concentrates, colorings, or extract. Each has a local name, too—the Criffel IPA, for instance, is christened after a local hill which can look like a massive mountain due to its lonely location. Another summit, Knockendoch, inspires a heavy ale that, aptly, will knock your socks off. Locals are typically found beside the brewery's bar (other than on Sundays, when it shuts), sipping the potions on draught, and guided tours operate at 1pm every Monday and Friday, concluding in Sulwath's shop.

---

209 King Street (+44 1556 504525, www.sulwathbrewers.co.uk)

▼ Born and bred in Naples, head chef Andrea's cooking at The Pheasant reflects his Italian upbringing.

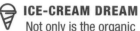
 CAFFEINE KICKS
In Dumfries itself, ***Kings*** began life as a Christian bookshop. It is still that but has morphed into a bigger space run by grind aficionados who travel to Melbourne, Australia, or Berlin, Germany, to further their passion. Most of the coffee hails from Has Bean, where baristas are also trained, although pour-overs sometimes use quirkier single origins. A longstanding gallery and emporium selling sculptures, ceramics, glass ornaments, bags, and jewelry, Castle Douglas's ***Designs*** also has a downstairs café. The homemade soups are good. The freshly baked breads and cakes are very good. And the Lavazza brews are positively lifesaving.

12 Queensberry Street (+44 1387 254444, www.kings-online.co.uk); 179 King Street (+44 1556 504552, www.designsgallery. co.uk)

ICE-CREAM DREAM
Not only is the organic ***Cream o' Galloway*** farm, near Lennox Plunton, well reputed for its gelatos and raw cheese, but it makes a brilliant day out for families, too. That's courtesy of a terrific adventure playground with tractors and trampolines, of farm tours and nature walks, of the inevitable ice cream parlor and, especially, of ice-cream tasting sessions (book in advance). As you cover 11 flavors, from raspberry and gingerbread to peppermint choc chip and sticky toffee, the production process is explained— including a rare (among dairy farms) ethical policy of letting calves stay with their mothers for five months.

Rainton, off A75 (+44 1557 814040, www.creamogalloway. co.uk)

BEST FEST
While June's Food Town Day involves visitors meeting producers and sellers, the calendar's biggest gastronomic event in CD is its ***Castle Douglas Harvest Food Festival***, held over a weekend in early September. Last year's headliner was *MasterChef: The Professionals* 2016 champion Gary MacLean, whose demo concluded a weekend of chocolate workshops, walk-in wine tastings, stalls, magicians, and music-and-drink festival. Farm machinery will be auctioned— do you need a plough?—and there may be a repeat of 2019's sausage-designing competition. The winning entry was produced by Ballards Butchers. Tickets start at £5.

www.facebook.com/ cdharvestfoodfest

 SUITCASE SWAG
If you come from the A74, stop near Annan at its ***Annandale Distillery***, not long reopened after 99 years out of action, and already a producer of acclaimed peated and unpeated single malt

◀ Cream o' Galloway is a deliciously fun place to visit, offering luxurious dairy ice cream, a woodland adventure playground, and miles of nature trails to explore.

world—and we really mean it. Along with the classic countries, you'll find potions from India, Lebanon, Romania, Japan (not sake), and Canada. As for tastings, these are themed to the season or a type of vino—sparkling, say—and cost from £10.

38 King Street (+44 7896 258440, www.thebottlelist.co.uk)

🍰 TEA TIME

As you may have already deduced, Castle Douglas is partial to a café. Another adjoins Threave Castle, a National Trust house and gardens just to the west, while two more suit tea-takers on, yup, King Street. Themed more toward canines (who are welcome) than Alice in Wonderland, the *Mad Hatter Café* cooks treacle scones and toasted teacakes alongside its breakfast and lunch menus and serves Earl Grey. Clumps of exposed brick await in the more dapper *Street Lights*, whose cakes are the main reason to visit. Choose from shortbread, banoffee, caramel, lemon drizzle, and more, all of them home-baked.

53 King Street (+44 1556 502712, www.cafescastledouglas.co.uk); 187 King Street (+44 1556 504222)

▲ The Bottle List has curated a range of wine from around the world that offers both value and quality.

whiskies. Continue on to Castle Douglas, whose *Irvings Homestyle Bakery* won a national gold award in 2019 for its custard creams. Then head further west again to another spirit maker, the gin-making *Crafty Distillery* in Newton Stewart. Though also new, it has also been plundering awards for potions using provincial botanicals like noble fir needles and bladder wrack. Along with a shop, guided tasting tours are offered, as at Annandale.

Northfield, off A75 (+44 1461 207817, www.annandaledistillery. com); Unit 1, Abercromby Industrial Park (+44 1556 504162, www. irvingsbakery.co.uk); Wigtown Road (+44 1671 404040, www. craftydistillery.com)

🍷 PERPETUAL WINE

The Bottle List came about in late 2017 after founder Chris Bain met with Ed Pook (see *Splash Out*) and devised a scheme to run recurrent tastings alongside Mr Pook's Kitchen, whose wines Bain oversees. Offering sage but non-pushy advice, his small shop is crammed with carefully chosen plonk from around the

Edinburgh

SCOLAND

> Though this book's predecessor featured Edinburgh, none
> of its tips will feature here—chiefly due to a tight-fisted
> hope that you'll buy both publications. Instead, here's a
whole new batch of suggestions, from pubs below Arthur's
Seat, supper clubs below Calton Hill, and Japanese gems, to
science tea shops and specialty coffee in a shopping mall.

ON A BUDGET?

Thought processes in Indian restaurants normally go something like this. 1: "Oh, that's cheap." 2: "Ohhh, it doesn't include rice." High fives, then, for *The Mosque Kitchen*, which negates the second part by pricing curry and rice from £6.50. Each dish's quality belies the plain canteen setting. If £6.50 is still too expensive, then a) you're flipping tight, and b) get yourself to *Oink's* Grassmarket outlet, where hog roast baps start at £3.95.

31–33 Nicolson Square (+44 131 6674035, www.mosquekitchen. com); 34 Victoria Street (+44 7771 968233, www.oinkhogroast.co.uk)

DATE FOR TWO

For decades, the small building afoot Calton Hill park was used by those responsible for the Royal Terrace Gardens. These days, however, *The Gardener's Cottage* is a magical, intimate restaurant of two dining rooms and three communal, supper club-like long tables, secluded away from Auld Reekie's perpetual hubbub. What's on the menu? No idea: food is simply provided in three- or six-course format, without options, based on what's seasonal and what fruit, vegetables, and herbs new gardener Charlie is harvesting in the front garden. Expect lots of flavor, though, and plenty of excitement for your taste buds.

1 Royal Terrace Gardens (+44 131 6770244, www.thegardenerscottage.co)

▼ There's no menu at The Gardener's Cottage. Dishes are a surprise for both the eyes and the taste buds.

SPLASH OUT

Stuart Ralston's new place, **_Noto_** is found in the New Town and is a New York City-inspired, Asian-obsessed venue whose sharing plates range from beef tartare alongside yuzu kosho and egg yolk, to fried buttermilk chicken with waffles and, what the hell, caviar. Fun? And then some. For the more traditionally inclined, West End's basement-set **_Forage & Chatter_** serves superior mushroom carpaccios and pork shoulders to guests sitting in elegant tweed booths.

47a Thistle Street (+44 131 241 8518, www.notoedinburgh.co.uk); 1a Alva Street (+44 131 225 4599, www.forageandchatter.com)

BRILL FOR BRUNCH

Praise be! Occupying the cozy, high-ceilinged ground floor of a converted church, **_Checkpoint_** is open all day but works best for brunch. Near the university on—useful for many Fringe-goers—Bristo Place, it adds blueberries, almonds, and honey overnight oats and piles more berries and naughty Chantilly cream atop brioche toast. Good eggs and fry ups tempt, too. Over in coastal Portobello, close to its sandy beach, **_The Skylark_** suggests toasted macadamia granola, borlotti bean stew on sourdough—that is, beans on toast 2:1—or porridge with good Ayrshire milk to clients of its white, sea chic café.

3 Bristo Place (+44 131 225 9352, www.checkpointedinburgh.com); 243 Portobello High Street (+44 131 629 3037, www.theskylark.co.uk)

▲ Checkpoint offers a buzzy, all-day dining experience, but their brunch comes highly recommended, so make sure to head over early.

LOCAL SECRET

The residential, rather classy district of Bruntsfield, south of Grassmarket and west of The Meadows, is exactly the sort of place where a local secret restaurant would hide—and so **Yamato** duly does. A sister Japanese joint to Kanpai, closer to the castle, its wide-ranging menu ticks off sushi, tempura, teppan, and lots of marbled wagyu beef, and is supplemented by various sakes. Veterans order the fatty tuna belly, the barbecued eel rice, or the hand-cut mountain yam noodles with aonori seaweed flakes and tempura sauce. If not already clear, this is unusual fare; better still, it's delivered with skill and flair.

11 Lochrin Terrace
(+44 131 466 5964,
www.yamatosushiedinburgh.co.uk)

KILLER COCKTAILS

In increasingly affluent Stockbridge, and ideally situated to conclude a Water of Leith walk—**The Last Word Saloon** is a lower key basement from the team behind revered subterranean Queen Street den Bramble. Its rugs, open fireplace, leather and, er, taxidermy squirrel conjure up an old-world feel, and so too do such warming, Prohibition-esque cocktails, such as Into the Pines—vodka, burnt sage, peat smoke, pine

▲ Nauticus champions Scottish produce where possible. Ninety percent of its products hail from the land of the brave or have links with the country.

◄ The Last Word Saloon offers cleverly constructed cocktails, including the lip smacking Best Kept Secret—two types of rum, Amandine liqueur, sherry, lime, and Irn Bru reduction.

oil, ginger, honey, and manzanilla sherry. Similarly cozy is Leith's **Nauticus**, whose cocktails champion Scottish production and the area's maritime heritage. Among them is Sweet Victory, combining Blackwoods vodka, bitters, rhubarb and lemongrass sorbet, and sparkling sherry.

44 St Stephen Street
(+44 131 225 9009,
www.lastwordsaloon.com);
142 Duke Street (+44 131 629
9055, www.nauticusbar.co.uk)

☕ CAFFEINE KICKS

The chain-tastic Waverley Mall, beside Edinburgh's main station, makes an unlikely venue for specialty coffee. That's part of the charm of **Williams & Johnson**, though; a much bigger part is their single-origin beans, seasonally chosen and freshly roasted over at Leith's flagship store. Soaring succulents and balsawood surfaces spawn a bright, welcoming esthetic. Over in the Old Town, meanwhile, **The Milkman** is an old sweetshop whose specialty UK-sourced espressos and flat whites vie for attention with Pekoe teas and hot chocolates using mixes by local artisans. Get a pick-me-up to go if you can't snag one of the window benches or tartan stools.

Waverley Mall, 3 Waverley Bridge (+44 131 557 3759, www.williamsandjohnson.com); 7 Cockburn Street (+44 777 207 7920, www.themilkman.coffee)

▼ The Milkman resides in an old sweetshop, serving house espresso sourced from the city itself and a range of rotating guest coffees.

🍰 TEA TIME

Imported around the world, **Eteaket's** loose-leaf blends also inform the brand's New Town tearoom. Staff bring not just your cuppa, but a timer so that infusion occurs for precisely the right duration. Cha-based cocktails, iced teas, and even tea lattes are also available, as are slices of cake plus afternoon, cream, and high teas, with fizz optional. Alternatively, tea flights—pairing five different blends with tea-infused chocolates—are offered at Eteaket's Concept Store, around the corner on Rose Street. Tea ware is also sold here, running to contemporary brewing equipment closer to chemistry sets than china pots.

41 Frederick Street (+44 131 226 2982, www.eteaket.co.uk)

🍷 PERPETUAL WINE

Plumly positioned beside the Water of Leith—with outside, riverside drinking perfectly acceptable—**Toast** is a relaxed "wine café" whose coffee, brunches, and imaginative Middle Eastern small plates all impress, but all take second billing behind a list of plonk ticking, mostly, the organic, natural, and biodynamic boxes. Such attributes are thoroughly *de rigueur*, but don't start envisioning this ex-gallery as a

soapbox for snobby folk; instead it is relaxed, welcoming, and pleasingly unpretentious. Back central, the Old Town's cool, cellar set *Divino Enoteca* uses a whizzy wine dispenser to divvy out glasses of fine Barbaresco, say, or Brunello di Montalcino.

65 Shore (+44 131 467 6984, www.toastleith.co.uk); 5 Merchant Street (+44 131 225 1770, www.vlttoriagroup.co.uk/divinoenoteca)

PUB PERFECTION

Previous visitors to *The Sheep Heid Inn* have included Queen Elizabeth II, Mary Queen of Scots (supposedly), and locals back in 1360, to when the Duddingston Loch village pub (supposedly) dates. They've also included numerous climbers of nearby

Arthur's Seat and anyone tempted by Scotland's oldest skittle alley, superb roasts, and an unexpectedly good gin range. Should scotch be more your bag, the central *Bow Bar* has 300 whiskies (as well as lots of craft and cask ale), while gastropub gluttons are directed to modern Scottish food from top chefs Tom Kitchin

and Dominic Jack at Stockbridge's *The Scran & Scallie*.

43–45 The Causeway (+44 131 661 7974, www.thesheepheid edinburgh.co.uk); 80 West Bow (+44 131 226 7667, www.thebowbar.co.uk); 1 Comely Bank Road (+44 131 332 6281, www.scranandscallie.com)

▶ Award-winning gastro pub, The Scran & Scallie creates menus showcasing great Scottish food—or "scran."

▼ The Bow Bar is among Edinburgh's finest whiskey destinations with more than 300 varieties on offer.

Aberdeen

and surrounding areas

SCOTLAND

> There's something stirring in northeast Scotland. Be it craft-beer crawls and bravura brunches in the "Granite City" itself, award-winning shortbread- and marmalade-makers nearby, Britain's best fish-and-chips scene, or a restaurant owned by Prince Charles, a fine gourmet offering is taking shape amid the glens, bens, castles, and clumps of Scots pine.

 ON A BUDGET?

This is a great area for fish and chips. **Low's Traditional,** in the otherwise unremarkable town of Westhill, seven miles from Aberdeen, came third in 2019's National Fish & Chip Awards, while the more attractive **Quayside Restaurant & Fish Bar** offers sea views in a simple room in Gourdon. Waiter service is available if you prefer to sit in, with crab cakes offering a menu twist. Inland, at the staid Deeside town of Banchory, the chic and esteemed Cowshed restaurant also operates a cheaper **Cowshed Chipper** takeaway. Portions of haddock or scampi with fries cost around £10.

Berryden Business Park (+44 1224 561212, www.lowstraditional. com); West Quay (+44 1561 360111, www.quaysidegourdon. co.uk); Raemoir Road (+44 1330 820813, www. cowshedrestaurantbanchory.co.uk)

 SPLASH OUT
Rothesay Rooms
was set up by Prince Charles after devastating flooding caused by Storm Frank damaged a large number of buildings in elegant Ballater. The result is a royal-standard restaurant. Amid racing-green walls and antler-horn candles, palpably Scottish dishes, such as short ribs with swede or hake enlivened by samphire and caviar abound with freshness and are presented with flourish. Far showier is Braemar's Fife Arms, which reopened in 2018 as a hotel by high-end gallerists Hauser & Wirth. Stunning art adorns every space: in **The Clunie Dining Room**, a wraparound Vorticist mural by Guillermo Kuitca can be admired between courses of turbot or birch-smoked venison.

3 Netherley Place (+44 1339 753816, www.rothesay-rooms.co. uk); Mar Road (+44 1339 720202, www.thefifearms.com)

◄ Eat on The Green creates good food using only the best local ingredients.

pleasure is always going to be better at source, right, where the relevant cows have long chewed their cud. As you'd expect, restaurants across Aberdeenshire serve the beef, but you'll be wanting somewhere good. Somewhere very good. So, try the cozy, low-ceilinged **Eat on The Green**, in quaint Udny Green where chargrilled fillets of Aberdeen Angus beef come with carrot purée, caramelized onions, a further beef cheek, triple-cooked chips, and pink-peppercorn cream.

Academy Court (+44 16 5184 2337, www.eatonthegreen.co.uk)

🍴 BRILL FOR BRUNCH

In Aberdeen itself, oil-workers, students, and everyone in-between congregates for brunch at **The Craftsman Company**, which is located steps from the station and Union Square shopping center. In a cozy room blending scrubbed floorboards, husks of original stonework, industrial piping, and chunky timber joins, an all-day menu features superlative Turkish eggs—essentially poached eggs with

🛢 PUB PERFECTION

Ask where you are at **The New Inn**—which isn't the least bit new—and villagers might well say "Foggieloan" (or simply "Foggie"). That's the old name for Aberchirder, one supplanted in, er, 1764. Such are the intriguing mysteries of a classic coaching halt where whiskies, wines, and cask ales accompany a stable-turned dining room serving pies and puddings. Upstairs are surprisingly chic, whitewashed rooms. To the south, in the highland games-hosting village of Oldmeldrum, **The**

Redgarth is similarly snug and relaxing—and has malts from neighboring Glen Garioch, one of Scotland's oldest whiskey distilleries.

79 Main Street (+44 1466 780633, www.newinnaberchirder.co.uk); Kirk Brae (+44 1651 872353, www.redgarth.com)

🍲 REGIONAL FAVES

Unlike, say, The Kinks, Blur, or Cliff Richard, Aberdeen Angus (or just Angus) cattle has made it big in America. That's thanks to its dense, marbled taste—and such palate-

Greek yogurt, chorizo oil, and sourdough toast—plus fluffy pancakes, bacon rolls, and smoothie bowls. High-quality produce is used and the coffee's excellent, too. After midnight, buckwheat risotto and lamb and goats' cheese croquettes with almond pesto join the party.

2 Guild Street (+44 1224 945600, www.thecraftsmancompany.com)

BEER OH BEER

These days, *BrewDog* operates over 70 international bars and even a craft-beer hotel in Ohio, midwest America. The company began in Aberdeenshire in 2007, in the port of Fraserburgh, and moved to their current whizzy premises in Ellon, north of Aberdeen, in 2012. Ninety-minute tours—or DogWalks—run daily (6pm on weekdays, and through the afternoon on weekends), and cover the old and newer brewhouses, the canning line, and head offices. There's also a taphouse on site, and sour-beer brewery called Overworks. If you're consigned to Aberdeen, the seven-stop craft beer kilometer (google it) features BrewDog bars and rival affairs.

Balmacassie Industrial Estate (+44 1358 724924, www.brewdog.com)

▼ BrewDog's state-of-the-art eco-brewery, north of Aberdeen, is one of the most technologically advanced in the world.

KILLER COCKTAILS

Aberdeen's exalted *Orchid* has been invited to send its staff to global competitions and has twice pocketed Cocktail Bar of the Year at the Scottish Licensed Trade News awards. It's a place which treats mixology reverentially, with its dozen drinks part-inspired by Professor Jerry Thomas' 1872 manual *How to Mix Drinks or the Bon Vivant's Companion*—considered the world's first cocktail book. Those 12 offerings include the sour Grannie's Smith, a fusion of gin, apple liqueur, bitters, egg white, lemon, and guava cordial. Mixology classes are also available upon request, as are gin and whiskey tastings.

---

51 Langstane Place (+44 1224 516126, www.orchidaberdeen. com)

CAFFEINE KICKS

There are now two branches of *The Coffee Apothecary*—one in Udny, rebooting a former Post Office, and their newer, sprucer joint near the BrewDog brewery in Ellon—all Scandi-style wood and straight lines. Coffee is taken very seriously, with Scotland's best small-batch roast beans prepared properly, including for pour-over filters. Cakes and lunches are available, too, while the Ellon branch also does burgers and schnitzels. Back in Aberdeen, on its northerly university campus, the living room-like *Kilau Coffee* has great black gold and exceptional brownies that derail many a diet.

---

21 The Square, Ellon (+44 1358 721946, www. thecoffeeapothecary.co.uk); 57–59 High Street (+44 1224 485510, www.kilaucoffee.com)

▼ At Orchid you can enjoy classic or contemporary cocktails mixed by skilled staff.

🧳 SUITCASE SWAG

An orange blend produced at Kincardine Castle—more of a turreted Victorian country house in truth—has won gold three years running at the Dalemain World Original Marmalade Awards. It's not available to buy onsite, but try the nearby **Finzean Farm Shop**, in heathery hills between Banchory and Aboync. Other worthy pit stops for supplies include NG Menzies Butchers (back inside the Cairngorms National Park at lovely Braemar) for haggis and Huntly shortbread-baker **Dean's**, whose Lizzie McCoo all-butter version has garnered national prizes. Buy it at the brand's café and gift shop.

Finzean Estate, off B976 (+44 1330 850710, www.finzean.com); Steven Road (+44 1466 792086 (www.deans.co.uk)

▲ Dean's Lizzie McCoo shortbread has won national prizes and the bakery sells it by the bucket load.

🎪 BEST FEST

Now two decades old, the one-day **Taste of Grampian** food and drink festival is held in elegant market town Inverurie in June. You can expect a reliable tranche of big-name cooks— last year saw *MasterChef* judge John Torode give a masterclass—and the best producers from across Grampian (of which Aberdeenshire is a part) selling their creamy fudge, smoked salmon, or malt whiskey. Musicians and magicians perform, too, and there's usually a cookery duel between two well-known kitchen amateurs. Entry last time round was £10 per adult, with under-16s going free; chef demos cost £8.

www.tasteofgrampian.co.uk

🥂 DATE FOR TWO

The former customs house on Aberdeen's quayside is now something much more exciting. Namely **The Silver Darling**, a laid-back restaurant whose upstairs floor-to-ceiling windows provide views of the harbor, the beach, the bay, and the fishing village of Footdee. If those soaring sea vistas don't do it for couples, perhaps a shareable seafood platter— starring oysters, mussels, and tiger prawns—will, or à la carte mains from venison and blackberry jus to ponzu-glazed cod. Failing all else, decadent desserts stand ready: warm cherry clafoutis served with homemade vanilla ice cream, Baileys and nutmeg crème brûlée, or lemon meringue cheesecake. Sorted.

Pocra Quay (+44 1224 576229, www.thesilverdarling.co.uk)

Bangor, Dundrum,
and surrounding areas

NORTHERN IRELAND

> Stretching south of Belfast, underrated County Down is spearheading the renaissance of both Northern Irish cuisine and produce. Its potatoes, butters, gins, oysters, and cheeses are superb, there are clever chefs and bargain prices everywhere, and the scenery—white sand beaches here, the moody Mourne Mountains there—is a sublime bonus. What's not to like?

💲 ON A BUDGET?

Down's shores, rivers, and vast Strangford Lough yield sensational salmon, bream, oysters, and mussels. One of the best places to tuck in is also one of the best value. In bayside village Dundrum, below a ruined Norman castle, the cozy *Mourne Seafood Bar* serves creamy chowders using each day's catch at just £7. For bargain breakfasts or lunches—plus a guaranteed warm welcome—consider heading north to Bangor, a resort town not far from Belfast. Everything in tiny café *The Drawing Room*, from haloumi fry ups to chili, chorizo, and chickpea casseroles to salted caramel donuts, mines local suppliers.

Main Street (+44 28 4375 1377, www.mourneseafood.com/dundrum); 21 Gray's Hill (+44 28 9147 8876, www.facebook.com/thedrawingroombangor)

🎊 BEST FEST

The royal family's official Northern Ireland residence is also home to Down's best epicurean bash. Run with BBC Good Food, the *Hillsborough Castle and Gardens Food Festival* only began life in 2019, yet still attracted big-name chefs, such as Nadiya Hussain and *The Doctor's Kitchen* author Rupy Aujla to its bandstand and live cookery demos over its early July weekend. Held in the government residence's beautiful 100-acre grounds, it also threw in stalls, kids' entertainment, bars, live musicians, a tasting theater, and castle tours.

---

www.hrpfoodfestivals.com/hillsborough-castle

▼ If you enjoy fresh local seafood at an affordable price then make your way to the Mourne Seafood Bar, whose shellfish is sourced from their very own shellfish beds.

PUB PERFECTION

Donaghadee, a port atop the Ards Peninsula, has history—it was once the "Gretna Green of Ireland" due to a boat taking elopers to Scotland—plus a lighthouse, a cool B&B, a gin and whiskey distillery, and *Grace Neill's*, supposedly Ireland's oldest pub. Quaff a pint of the black stuff in snugs dating back to 1611, then head to *Balloo House*, just west of Strangford Lough, to try nosh awarded Michelin's Bib Gourmand for quality and affordability. Fine local beef and venison inform pub classic mains gone posh, while the pudding choices are led by whiskey-soaked bread and butter puddings.

33 High Street (+44 28 9188 4595, www.graceneills.com); 1 Comber Road, Killinchy (+44 28 9754 1210, www.ballooinns.com/balloo-house)

CAFFEINE KICKS

Specialty coffee can increasingly be found in Down, as the scene filters (sorry) south from Dublin. In Newtownards, on Strangford Lough's northern tip and not far from the lonely Scrabo Tower, gallery café *Haptik* expertly puts guest roasts—April and Round Hill among them—through a spearmint-colored La Marzocco machine, and serves brunch to boot. Just down the lough, Comber's *Trait Coffee* is a cool, sparse end-of-terrace cube where Root & Branch grind accompanies hot choc by local artists NearyNógs. And in Saintfield, seven miles southwest, *Tribe Coffee* blends mud from local roaster Ristretto amid converted forge's horsebox, next to the village's Saturday market.

29 Frances Street (+44 28 9182 1039, www.wearehaptik.com); 33 Castle Street (www.facebook.com/traitcoffee); 68e Main Street (+44 7825 077797, www.instagram.com/tribe.coffee)

◀ Balloo House is a cozy, country pub with dining in the bar downstairs and weekend dining in the wood-fired grill restaurant upstairs.

🍰 TEA TIME

Slieve Donard serves a posh afternoon tea, as does *The Old Inn* at Crawfordsburn, west of Bangor. A thatched, seventeenth-century hostelry turned boutique hotel, it accompanies award-winning modern European dinners and suits of armor with fireside teas in the Parlour Bar. Expect finger sandwiches, sponges, scones, tea infusions, and fine china as standard. More informal are the Riverside Tea Rooms, next to the Lagan in Dromore, and the *Eden Pottery* studio's cafe, where hot raspberry and white chocolate scones and coffee and walnut cakes are the order of most days. Jews were protected during the World Wars in surrounding seaside town Millisle.

Main Street (+44 28 9185 3255, www.theoldinn.com); 218 Abbey Road (+44 28 9186 2300, www.edenpotteryshop.co.uk)

🍴 BRILL FOR BRUNCH

A village in Down's northwest corner, Moira dates back over a millennia and a half. A piffling 140 years old is its butchers, *McCartney's of Moira*, and newer still is the cheery, two-floor café next door. The former's success—with national titles for its pork sausages and corned beef—

▲ One of the oldest family butchers in Northern Ireland, McCartney's of Moira has won national titles for its famous corned beef.

inspired the latter, which uses this acclaimed fodder in superior brunch plates, like hash with poached eggs or sausage pancake stacks. A few lighter veggie dishes are also offered. Back in Dundrum, however, the popular and family run *Blue Bay Café* and Bakery has lots of vegan options, from sausage sandwiches to carrot cake.

56–62 Main Street (+44 28 9261 1422, www.mccartneysofmoira. com); 105 Main Street (+44 28 4375 1283, www.facebook.com/ bluebaycafeandbakery)

▲ The Slieve Donard Hotel and Spa houses the Oak Restaurant, which allows residents to dine in style and enjoy fabulous food.

SPLASH OUT

Not content with a plum position between Dundrum Bay's white sand and those Mourne Mountains, small resort Newcastle boasts the area's most exciting restaurant. At seafront *Brunel's*, Paul Cunningham takes local produce and wizards it into whey cooked lamb, hay-smoked venison, gin-cured trout with seaweed gel, or sea buckthorn curd with shards of fennel meringue. Also good, and only a few minutes away is the *Oak Restaurant* at posh Victorian country house hotel Slieve Donard, which abuts the acclaimed Royal County Down Golf Club. Amid wood-paneled, fire-heated finery, it serves shorthorn beef rumps and raspberry parfaits with white chocolate ganache.

32 Downs Road (+44 28 4372 3951, www.brunelsrestaurant. co.uk); Downs Road (+44 28 4372 1066, www.hastingshotels.com/ slieve-donard-resort-and-spa)

SUITCASE SWAG

Two County Down cheesemakers have led Northern Ireland's *fromage* revolution. Paul McClean began making semi-hard Kearney Blue from his Irish sea-facing cottage in 2010, and has since been feted at the International Cheese Awards; and Mike Thomson's raw milk blue Young Buck, first developed in 2012 (as Mike's Fancy Cheese), is now hawked in Michelin-starred European restaurants. You'll find both at Comber's *Indie Fude* shop, along with charcuterie and preserves. The same town's Comber Early potatoes, spuds with a distinct nutty flavor and Protected Geographical Indication (PGI) status, are sold at the *Ashvale Farm Shop*, near Lisburn—as are honeys and homemade pies.

30 Castle Street (+44 28 9122 6359, www.indiefude.com); Ashvale House, 11 Old Ballynahinch Road (+44 28 9263 8099, www.ashvalefarmshop. co.uk)

REGIONAL FAVES

Van Morrison's nostalgic spoken word song "Coney Island," recalls childhood journeys around Down and includes a foodie memory of stopping off at Ardglass for mussels and potted herrings. Ardglass, a fishing village, was long famed for its herring, but stock reductions and other factors mean very little is found there now—and the shop Van visited is long gone. But *McKeown's*, a fishmonger in Bangor might have some—ring up to check.

14 High Street (+44 28 9127 1141, www.mckeownsfishmongers. co.uk)

🚏 ON THE TRAIL

Unsure where to start? Then start with *NI Food Tours*, whose director Tracey Jeffery can arrange bespoke coach or car circuits. What you see is your choice, but Tracey can arrange special access to producers of those PGI-protected Comber Early

potatoes, elite oyster beds, Kilmegan cider, Shortcross gin, and many more. Guests of ***Enniskeen Country House Hotel*** near Newcastle can also undertake self-guided, all downhill "Mourne Food & Films Cycle Tours," whose rural stops range from "Game of Thrones'" locations to meetings

▶With NI Food Tours, sample local produce, such as single-estate whiskey, artisan bread, and fresh fish straight off the boat.

▼ Enjoy afternoon tea on the terrace at Enniskeen Country House Hotel.

with the makers of hand-churned Abernethy Butter— used by Heston— before an afternoon tea.

52a Ballymorran Road (+44 28 9754 3224, www. nifoodtours.com); 98 Bryansford Road (+ 44 28 4372 2392, www.enniskeenhotel.co.uk)

Belfast

NORTHERN IRELAND

> As if it needs saying, but there's so much more to Belfast than Guinness. Specifically, pear wood oven brasseries, bargain-priced boutiques, Narnia-themed cafés, samurai-principled Asian restaurants, AeroPress champions, leafy rooftop cocktail dens, chorizo tacos, curio-filled folks pubs, Hibernian hotpots, and vanilla pecan donuts.

ON A BUDGET?

A snazzy boutique hotel off Shaftesbury Square in the busy Golden Mile area, **Benedicts** offers impecunious visitors two handy solutions. Firstly, rock up to its grand bar just after 4pm to enjoy happy-hour rates when every cocktail costs £4. After a couple of those, head to the vaulted, low-ceiling restaurant to capitalize on a Beat the Clock menu: between 5 and 7pm every day, most dishes are available for £7. They include steak and Guinness pie, peppered pork fillets, and a vegan tomato tagine. With happy hour continuing until 10pm, there's even time to nip back to the bar for another.

7–21 Bradbury Place (+44 28 9059 1999, www.benedictshotel.co.uk)

SPLASH OUT

Belfast's biggest-name chef, Michael Deane, owns and oversees seven restaurants in the city. The fanciest, and his flagship, is Michelin-starred **Deanes EIPIC**, named after the food-loving Greek philosopher Epicurus. Promoting local fare, this contemporary restaurant serves tasting menus of varying lengths, for meat eaters and vegetarians alike. Among the standout dishes is fine Wicklow venison accompanied by carrot, sorrel, and potato boulangère. Rather cooler is **EDÕ**, a new brasserie from Gordon Ramsay protégé Jonny Elliott. Distinctively cooked using a smoky, apple, and pear wood Bertha oven, his European-style dishes are typified by taramasalata and chorizo on toast, and beef cheeks with cauliflower.

BRILL FOR BRUNCH

Ormeau Road is a gentrifying area of South Belfast where shabby River Lagan-side warehouses are becoming pricey flats, and nu-ramen bars neighbor pawn shops. You know the type. An early adopter was *General Merchants*, whose brunch menu delivers Earl Grey bircher muesli, huevos rotos, and pea fritters with labneh, sumac, poached eggs, and pistachios amid varnished wood fittings and crisp white walls. If that sounds far too millennial, head east instead and hole up at *The Lamppost Café*, where frescoes herald local legend CS Lewis and his *Chronicles of Narnia*. A Sunday brunch menu stars savory waffles and brioche baps.

▲ It's no surprise that Deanes EIPIC has a Michelin star—it consistently delivers the freshest and most seasonal produce cooked to perfection.

28–40 Howard Street (+44 28 9033 1134, www.deaneseipic. com); Capital House, 3 Upper Queen Street (+44 28 9031 3054, www.edorestaurant.co.uk)

PUB PERFECTION

Belfast is full of ornate pubs and bars dating back to the Victorian era. *The Crown Liquor Saloon*, a gas-lit, National Trust owned gin palace, scores most headlines, but equally charismatic is *Kelly's Cellars*. Open since 1720 and little changed since, its timeworn bar and curio-filled arches host folk musicians four times a week and serve one of the city's best pints of Guinness. Folk music

also awaits at *Sunflower*, a recent revamp of a longstanding pub whose security grille reminds us of this city's worst days. As well as musicians every night, you'll find a good range of craft beers and much craic.

46 Great Victoria Street (+44 28 9024 3187, www.nicholsonspubs. co.uk); 30–32 Bank Street (+22 28 9024 6058, www.kellyscellars. co.uk); 65 Union Street (+44 28 9023 2474, www.sunflowerbelfast. com)

▶ Enjoy a ceili (Irish dance) at the Sunflower, with live music played every night.

361 Ormeau Road (+44 28 9029 1007, www.generalmerchants. co.uk/ormeau-road); 9 Upper Newtownards Road (+44 28 9058 0080, www.thelamppostcafe.com)

REGIONAL FAVES

Artefacts and peat fires aren't the only traditional touches at **Whites**, which dates back to 1630 and reckons to be Belfast's oldest tavern. Nope, you'll also find classic Hibernian dishes such as seafood chowder, Irish stew—a meat and root vegetable hotpot whose exact ingredients, as with all folk dishes, are contentious—and steak and Guinness pie. Not that it's all bygone: summer sees a free courtyard cinema with complimentary chicken wings. But we digress; have you ever had a boxty? A traditional potato pancake, it's served at **Holohan's Pantry** and done differently each day: with bacon, say, or perhaps creamy prawns.

2–4 Winecellar Entry (+44 28 9031 2582, www.whitestavernbelfast. com); 43 University Road (+44 28 9029 1103, www.holohanspantry. co.uk)

CAFFEINE KICKS

Staff from **Established Coffee**, a sharp spot in the Cathedral Quarter, have won domestic AeroPress championships, and have V60 and Chemex machines at their disposal. Suffice to say they know what they're doing. The beans hail from roasters such as Origin and Calendar, and there's also a wacky brunch menu extending to house made chocolate milk with cinnamon and beer and cheese baps. Those minded towards combining little snacks and long blacks are also directed to **Guilt Trip** out east. There are two central provisions here: single-origin, pour-over brews prepared with love, and donuts—from cinnamon to vanilla pecan—handmade fresh that morning.

54 Hill Street (www.established. coffee); 4 Orangefield Lane (www. guilttripcoffee.com)

LOCAL SECRET

"Traditional Asian styles of cooking with a Belfast bushidō attitude," is how **Yugo** describes itself; bushidō being a chivalric samurai code. Hidden on the side of City Hall in a narrow, brick and wood bar, it serves unusual wonders: dry-aged beef rumps with wombok, truffle and egg, lamb shoulder massamans, or wok-fried green beans next to spicy pork mince. Just as popular, and revered, are Mexican joint **Boojum's** five branches, chiefly thanks to sensational burritos containing super tender meat, tomato-based rice, and rich salsa, plus rare ingredients like achiote paste and annatto seeds. Look out for the chorizo tacos, too.

◀ A casual Mexican burrito bar, Boojum offers award-winning food at affordable prices.

▶ All of the wines at Ox Cave wine bar are available by the glass, which is quite a treat. Enjoy with a side of cheese and charcuterie.

3 Wellington Street (+44 28 9031 9715, www.yugobelfast.com); 14–16 Great Victoria Street (+44 28 9023 3200, www.boojummex.com)

 ## KILLER COCKTAILS

Ascend five storeys in a clanking, thoroughly old-school lift and you'll find skylights, birdcages, brick walls, and huge pot plants. Welcome to *The Perch*, a rooftop Linen Quarter bar and terrace styled like a secret garden. You'll find pizzas, DJs at night, and cool cocktails served in pots. An unusual Carolina Wren combines Northern Irish whiskey from Bushmills with cream soda and apricot creme. Dimmer and more mysterious is *Love & Death Inc*, where waxy candelabra and a retro bike hanging from the rafters await. So, too, do Belfast's best cocktails, exemplified by the Berrito: Bacardi, mint and, yes, a whole Berocca tablet.

42 Franklin Street (+44 28 9024 8000, www.facebook.com/theperchbelfast); 10a Ann Street (+44 28 9024 7222, www.facebook.com/loveanddeathbelfast)

DATE FOR TWO

Holohan's (see *Regional Faves*) also has a sister outpost floating on the Lagan. Moored beside the Hall, candlelit *Holohan's at the Barge* comes with attractive views of Queen's Bridge. Those same boxties are available along with seafood chowders or venison beside a chocolate jus. If you don't stare into your lover's eyes, gaze at them in *The Ginger Bistro*, handily close to the Grand Opera House and, using Irish produce, a purveyor of simple but superb dishes. Epitomizing them are pan-roasted, ham wrapped chicken breasts in a mushroom, bacon, and red wine gravy, plus buttery cabbage and cheddar mash.

1 Lanyon Quay (+44 28 9023 5973, www.holohansatthebarge. co.uk); 68–72 Great Victoria Street (+44 28 9024 4421, www.gingerbistro.com)

PERPETUAL WINE

Neighboring the seasonal menu of the highly regarded Ox restaurant and on the Lagan, the dark wood *Ox Cave* wine bar serves mostly local cheese and charcuterie. But those are merely garnishes to a high-quality tipple list blending old-world classics with those of forgotten grapes or new, artisan, and biodynamic vintages. All are available by the glass, and friendly staff will happily advise. Wine tastings are held once a month on Thursdays, usually led by winemakers or specialists, and there's live music most Saturdays from 9pm. Ask if you can see some Valyrian steel knives that were used in "Game of Thrones."

3 Oxford Street (+44 28 9023 2567, www.oxbelfast.com/ox-cave)

Betws-y-Coed, Menai Bridge,

and surrounding areas

WALES

> Anchored by Snowdonia, Wales' top corner has seen free-thinking restaurateurs and quality producers emerge in recent years, helped by the area's terrific geography. From Anglesey to Aberystwyth via the Llŷn Peninsula, Conwy Castle, and Colwyn Bay, this corner offers ample gourmet compensation to go with its tourist trains, zip wires, and mountain treks.

ON A BUDGET?

At the foot of Wales' highest peak, lakeside village Llanberis is the outdoor-activities hub of Snowdonia—and a starting point for railway rides up to the 1,085-meter summit. Train-trippers, hikers, and fell-runners fond of cheap eats congregate at *Pete's Eats*, a cheerily decorated caff open since 1978. In recent times it has earned awards and blogger acclaim for beef burger rolls (£3) or cheese and chip butties (£3.50). All-day veggie grills are £6.50. Chips are homemade from Maris piper potatoes and there's a range of daily soups and specials. Bunkhouse accommodation awaits upstairs.

40 High Street (+44 1286 870117, www.petes-eats.co.uk)

SPLASH OUT

As the name suggests, Michelin-starred *Sosban & The Old Butcher's* occupies a former meat store. In Menai Bridge, just onto the Isle of Anglesey, it also delivers a "culinary journey" via inventive tasting menus, which focus on Welsh produce. Dishes depend on what's available each day. With opening hours limited to Thursday through Saturday nights, booking well ahead is essential. The mainland's best bet is *Craig-y-Dderwen*, a luxury

Betws-y-Coed hotel, and its River Conwy-facing restaurant. Supported by a wine cellar, dishes here again champion provincial fare—epitomized by poached Anglesey eggs on a leek bed beside Carmarthen ham and cheese.

Trinity House, 1 High Street (+44 1248 208131, www.sosbanandtheoldbutchers.com); Betws-y-Coed (just off A5) (+44 1690 710293, www.snowdoniahotel.com/restaurant.htm)

PUB PERFECTION

West of Snowdonia the Llŷn Peninsula stretches 30 miles into the Irish Sea. Halfway along its northern edge, near Morfa Nefyn, a lush finger extends briefly northward, encompassing only a lifeboat station, a sandy beach, a fishing hamlet behind it called Porthdinllaen, and, in that, the *Ty Coch Inn*. Accessible only on foot—a 20-minute walk across the Nefyn & District Golf Course— this secluded charmer occupies an old, vicarage building and serves specials, pies, potatoes, and paninis each day from 12–2.30pm. Sit outside, if possible, and gaze toward the awesome Snowdonia.

Porthdinllaen (+44 1758 720498, www.tycoch.co.uk)

BRILL FOR BRUNCH

Also a food shop and gallery space, *Idris Stores'* café is firmly in the "hidden gem" category. Found in pine-swathed Corris, an attractive old slate-mining village on the Snowdonia park's southern tip, it particularly majors in brunch. "Saturday Club" diners can scoff freshly made frittatas, burritos, chickpea pancakes or omelettes, and bacon on sourdough toast—with lots of choice for vegans and vegetarians—while scones and delectable brownies are always available. The coffee, made to a barista-like standard, is also exceptional. Nearby is a narrow-gauge railway and the subterranean King Arthur's Labyrinth attraction.

Bridge Street (www.facebook.com/idrisstores)

REGIONAL FAVES

Concocted from flour, butter, eggs, milk, and currants, Welshcakes are similar to scones, but cooked on a griddle. The original version is lovely (especially hot), but today's artisans have also been introducing lemon, Irish cream liqueur, mint chocolate, and cranberry and orange-flavored varieties. One such place is *Popty Conwy*, a bakery in the castle town. Further northwest, the Menai Strait

▲ Offering unrivaled views of The Rivals mountain range, the Ty Coch Inn is one of Wales' top beach bars accessible only by foot.

produces half of the UK's mussels and you can try them steamed in white wine, shallots, garlic, and cream at *Dylan's*. Of this innovative modern dining brand's three outposts, its timber-clad Menai Bridge branch is the coziest and offers fine harbor vistas.

4 Castle Street (+44 1492 581004, www.facebook.com/conwybakery); St George's Road (+44 1248 716714, www.dylansrestaurant. co.uk)

▲ Welshcakes are a local delicacy not too dissimilar to scones. Pick up these regional favorites in Popty Conwy, who have introduced new flavors to these traditional treats.

🍺 BEER OH BEER

As well as being the terminus point of the chugging Ffestiniog Railway, riverside town Porthmadog—known locally as "Port," and just east of the Llŷn Peninsula—is home to the *Purple Moose*, a 40-barrel microbrewery with plenty of admirers. Among their award-winning wares are IPAs, a chocolate-infused stout, and the top-selling Snowdonia Ale, a light golden charmer. Brewery tours operate only on Wednesdays, but recently added taproom pub The Australia and bottle shop Siop y Bragdy (Mon–Fri), both on Porthmadog's white-hued High Street, stay open for longer.

Madoc Street (+44 1766 515571, www.purplemoose.co.uk)

☕ CAFFEINE KICKS

On the North Wales coast, elegant Victorian resort town Llandudno is most famous for its classic pleasure pier. Coffee hounds however, know it for *Providero*, whose outposts—a cooler one on central Mostyn Street and a smaller original in Llandudno Junction—manipulate freshly roasted specialty beans. More than 30 blends of loose-leaf tea and gourmet hot chocolates are offered, too, as are cakes, and, at the newer branch, breakfast and lunch. Over on Cardigan Bay, all those university

students pulling all-nighters in Aberystwyth need caffeine, and *Sophie Bach* serves some of the best. Doggie donuts and "pawsecco" are available for pups as well.

112 Upper Mostyn Street (+44 1492 338220, www.facebook. com/providero); 13 Cambrian Place (+44 7432 252671, www. facebook.com/sophiebachcafe)

🧳 SUITCASE SWAG

At its slate-mining peak, Blaenau Ffestiniog was North Wales' second-largest town. With the industry long since moved on, this uplands town now relies chiefly on tourism. Another new commerce is cheese-making, with South Caernarfon Creameries aging its award-winning Dragon cheddar within the *Llechwedd* slate caverns attraction. Buy blocks in its gift shop, then drive north to castle town Conwy and trawl *Baravelli's* for exquisite "bean to bar" chocolates handmade by married couple Emma and (the elaborately mustachioed) Mark. So esteemed are these that Harrods has stocked the pair's artisan Easter eggs.

Slate Mountain (+44 1766 830306, www.llechwedd.co.uk); 13 Bangor Road (+44 1492 330540, www. baravellis.com)

DATE FOR TWO

Wales' best-known contemporary chef? It might just be Bryn Williams, who shot to *Great British Menu* fame and now oversees London restaurants in Primrose Hill and Somerset House. And also, ***Bryn Williams at Porth Eirias***, beside the beach in Colwyn Bay and 15 miles north of Williams' home town Denbigh. Floor-to-ceiling glass windows render it a tremendously romantic spot. Book a good table and watch the waves or the sunset as you try roasted prawns with garlic, chili, and seaweed mayonnaise or a brilliant baked Alaska. Seafood is a focus and three courses typically cost a very reasonable £35.

The Promenade (+44 1492 577525, www.portheirias.com)

TEA TIME

Tu Hwnt i'r Bont is certainly eye-catching. A former timber cottage swathed in Virginia creeper—which turns a blazing crimson hue in fall—beside the low-humped Pont Fawr bridge (supposedly designed by Inigo Jones) and rushing River Conwy just across from Llanrwst. Devourable in an outdoor garden, its calorific cream teas and fruity bara brith bread also earn mostly good reviews, but less so the service. For a surer thing, decamp south, staying on Snowdonia's fringes, to the luxury country-house hotel ***Palé Hall***. Afternoon teas here, available from 3–5pm, feature fine-quality brews, vintage china stacks, and torpor-inducing armchairs.

Pont Fawr (+44 1492 642322, www.tuhwntirbont.co.uk); Palé Estate, Llandderfel (+44 16 7853 0285, www.palehall.co.uk)

An afternoon tea at Palé Hall is a feast of pure indulgence with a selection of finger sandwiches, assorted cakes, fruit and plain scones, and endless cups of tea or glasses of fizz.

Abergavenny

WALES

> Monmouthshire's main town is tempting as it is, what with the fine Norman church and cool shopping, the ruined castle on its fringes, and the fine Brecon Beacons and Black Mountains walks awaiting just beyond. Throw in punch-above-their-weight restaurants and Britain's best food festival however, and Abergavenny becomes near-irresistible.

BEST FEST
The ace up Abergavenny's sleeve? Easy: its annual mid-September gastro weekend, now 21 years old and liable to lure 30,000 attendees. So, what exactly makes the *Abergavenny Food Festival* one of the UK's best? Firstly, its star power, with previous editions luring the likes of Skye McAlpine and Hugh Fearnley-Whittingstall. Then its variety of offerings: fete-style stalls and workshops, sure, but also demos in the ruined castle, foraging walks for kids,

markets, and parties. Finally, Abergavenny puts an admirable emphasis on conscience and current affairs. For instance, 2019 witnessed Asma Khan, of Netflix's *Chef's Table* fame, discussing #MeToo's effect on the hospitality industry.

www.abergavennyfoodfestival.com

▼ Abergavenny Food Festival draws in some of the culinary world's most famous faces while also showcasing the rising stars emerging from the industry.

ON A BUDGET?

If you've ever been described as an epicurean, **Wendy's Cafe** probably won't do it for you. But if honest nosh, friendly service, and daily specials have you nostalgically tearing up with happiness, this lunch caff is the place. From aptly named "mega breakfasts," available all day for £7.50, to homemade lasagne, a side, chips, and a drink for £7, value abounds. Everything is well cooked and no dietary requirement—gluten-free, lactose-intolerant, vegan, or veggie—is ever received with a scowl. Other places in Abergavenny might do loftier cuisine, yet nowhere will make you feel as welcome.

Lion House, King Street (+44 1873 854000, www.facebook.com/pg/wendyscafe16)

SPLASH OUT

There have been bumpy times at **The Walnut Tree Inn**; bumpiest of all was a 2004 appearance on *Ramsay's Kitchen Nightmares*.

But ever since Shaun Hill arrived its fortunes have improved drastically. Now Michelin-starred, the inn—which also has hotel rooms and sits two miles east of town where the Black Mountains and Brecon Beacons converge—serves diners in a low-lit, art-filled room. There's no overriding gastronomic style, but key focuses are British ingredients and a frippery-free wholesomeness: see the cod with clams, chanterelles, bacon, and hazelnuts, or pork loins alongside Boston baked beans and cabbage.

Llanddewi Skirrid (+44 1873 852797, www.thewalnuttreeinn.com)

▼ There's plenty of choice at The Hardwick; its comprehensive menu covers everything from small plates to Sunday roasts.

 PUB PERFECTION
Stephen Terry, *The Hardwick's* head chef, used to work for Marco Pierre White and Michel Roux Jr—meaning that the latter's pronouncement that this is his favorite Welsh gastropub can be heard with a pinch of salty bias. Factor in *Good Hotel Guide* acclaim though and doubters should be convinced. If not, just visit the cozy den on Abergavenny's southern fringe and try something delicious from the ultra-extensive menus. Local game, from Brecon lamb to Herefordshire pork, is a staple. For something less distinguished—read: cheaper—the town center *Grofield Inn* has CAMRA- (the Campaign for Real Ale) approved ales and a sizeable beer garden.

Old Raglan Road (+44 1873 854220, www.thehardwick.co.uk); Baker Street (+44 1873 858939, www.grofield.com)

SUITCASE SWAG
Tempting boutiques litter Abergavenny's center, but none is more dangerous than *The Marches Delicatessen*. Numerous Welsh producers are represented here, from NomNom chocolate (look out for an Espresso Martini flavor) to the jam-making Preservation Society, and everything from salami to seaweed-spiced rum

is on sale. The biggest focus though is cheese, with the soft, cider washed Golden Cenarth especially worth investigation. Turn up Cibi Walk's arches and you'll pass brownie specialist *Chock Shop*, whose varieties include Irish cream liqueur and, amen, sticky toffee pudding. Should you catch the whiff of a freshly baked batch, resistance is entirely pointless.

16 Nevill Street (+44 1873 268080, www.marchesdeli.co.uk); 1 Cibi Walk, off Frogmore Street (+44 7885 697139, www.chockshop.co.uk)

▲ Chock Shop's famous artisan brownies—which are handmade, hand-cut, and hand decorated—cause queues at their shop, at food festivals, and at food markets up and down the country.

🍴 BRILL FOR BRUNCH

Cwtch means two things in Welsh: a cuddle and a cozy place. The latter perfectly describes the *Cwtch Cafe*, whose charming service and homemade food have earned nationwide repute. There's no shortage of all-day options for brunchers, from lemon meringue pie to fluffy American-style pancakes and poached eggs to mushrooms on toast. Yet, ultimately, there's really only one option: a superlative Welsh rarebit, done here with a mustard kick (although you can request otherwise). Coffees and cakes stand by if needed and prices are preposterously good; the rarebit, for instance, is just £6.

58 Cross Street
(+44 1873 855466)

DATE FOR TWO

Pre-request a secluded table at *Casa Bianca* and you should get your wish. It's part of an ultra-attentive service style that marks out this Italian bistro. So, too, does its food, from cheesy, moreish calzone to tomahawk pork chops or chargrilled swordfish in lemon and butter sauce. They also do a top-notch tiramisu. If it's too busy—booking is advised—or you fancy something quirkier, consider supper at the *Art Shop & Chapel's* crypt café. These are only available when there's an Americana or soul concert in the nineteenth-century chapel. Nicely cooked seasonal dishes using garden-plucked fare are the norm and you must reserve.

---

51 Frogmore St (+44 1873 737744, www.casabianca.co.uk); Market Street (+44 1873 736430, www.artshopandgallery.co.uk)

TEA TIME

There's lots to like about *The Angel Hotel*. It has plenty of local art, a bakery, an award-winning wine list, and does decent cocktails, too. Snug but pale-hued rooms befit a nineteenth-century inn gone slightly cool. Plus, it does Abergavenny's very best high and afternoon teas: decadent, diet-destroying affairs of savory sandwiches, warm scones, strawberry jam, mini pastries, and more, with bottles of prosecco on standby if needed. High tea also comes with a selection of fine teas so good

▼ Artisan bread is one of the many food offerings on sale at the Angel Bakery, which is located right next to The Angel Hotel.

that the Tea Guild itself has previously bestowed The Angel with its top award.

15 Cross Street
(+44 1873 857121,
www.angelabergavenny.com)

 **CAFFEINE KICKS**
Not only is *Fig Tree Espresso*—operating from a handsome Georgian townhouse—an independent shop, but its young owners, Jessica and Chris, use arabica java that's freshly roasted and packed each week just 30 minutes away at Ross-on-Wye's artisan James Gourmet Coffee company. Expect a rich chocolate and nut flavor profile. And expect to encounter a dangerous array of cakes: over 500 have been offered so far, from apricot Bakewell tart to apple and peanut butter gateau. Soups and salads are also served come lunchtime.

15 Nevill Street (www.abergavennycoffee.co.uk)

▲ Located right in the heart of town, Abergavenny Market is a lively and bustling fair offering the best locally produced products.

 **MARKET RESEARCH**
On Cross Street is *Abergavenny Market's* historic hall, its caramel bricks and arched windows giving way to a spacious interior of red-and-black chequerboard floors and bright blue pipes. Life-sized animal impersonations—which were produced for the festival one year—hang down from the roof. A general market, selling everything from t-shirts and truffles to honeys and haberdashery, runs on Tuesdays, Fridays, and Saturdays (except the second Saturday of every month, when it is given over to crafts) from 9am through 5pm. Another good fair for foodies is the artisan market, but this only occurs the fourth Thursday of every month between 9am and 2.30pm.

Cross Street (+44 1873 735811, www.facebook.com/abergavennymarket)

Index

ACKNOWLEDGMENTS

The publishers would like to thanks the restaurants, press agencies, and tourist boards who took the time to answer questions and provide images for inclusion in the book.

PICTURE CREDITS

KEY TO SYMBOLS

 SPLASH OUT
Based on a design by Nakul Dhaka from the Noun Project

 BRILL FOR BRUNCH
Created by Mello from the Noun Project

 SUITCASE SWAG
Created by monkik from the Noun Project

DATE FOR TWO
Created by Adrien Coquet from the Noun Project

 CAFFEINE KICKS
Based on a design by Viktor Minuvi from the Noun Project

 MARKET RESEARCH
Based on a design by Ayesha Rana from the Noun Project

 ON A BUDGET
Created by Icon Solid from the Noun Project

 PUB PERFECTION
Created by AomAm from the Noun Project

 LOCAL SECRET
Created by hunotika from the Noun Project

 BEST FEST
Created by Made x Made from the Noun Project

 REGIONAL FAVES
Based on a design by Arthur Shlain from the Noun Project

 PERPETUAL WINE
Based on a design by Alex Furgiuele from the Noun Project

KILLER COCKTAILS
Created by Jony from the Noun Project

 BEER OH BEER
Created by Paul Tilby

 ICE CREAM DREAM
Based on a design by Vectors Market from the Noun Project

 ON THE TRAIL
Created by Iconfactory Team from the Noun Project

 TEA TIME
Based on a design by Edward Boatman from the Noun Project